"I have never seen or heard of an excellent school that did not have an excellent principal. In this important new book McLaughlin helps us to understand what it takes to become a genuine expert as a school leader by closely examining how they navigate the challenges involved in leading schools during these turbulent times. For policymakers, district leaders, parents and others who want to see more progress in the effort to improve our nation's schools, this book will be an invaluable resource."

—Pedro A. Noguera, PhD
Peter L. Agnew Professor of Education
Steinhardt School of Culture, Education and Development
Executive Director, Metropolitan Center for
Research on Equity and the Transformation of Schools
New York University

"This book is a rare blend of practice and solid academic work. Dionne V. McLaughlin's writing shows that she 'talks the talk because she has walked the walk.' As a former elementary and secondary school site administrator with a multicultural background, she navigates some of the most difficult and dangerous waters in school site decision making today. In the process of unpacking the nature of difficult decisions, she has not only created powerful exemplars that others can follow, but has erected models that will serve as fount of motivation and inspiration."

—Fenwick W. English
R. Wendell Eaves Senior
Distinguished Professor of Educational Leadership
School of Education
The University of North Carolina at Chapel Hill

"Agile and inspiring principals remain key to lifting America's schools, to accelerate our progress in narrowing disparities in student learning. Dionne V. McLaughlin vividly describes the everyday challenges that face principals—coaching mediocre teachers, trying to engage dissident kids, inspiring teachers to collaborate and labor as eager professionals. It's a masterful volume, offering ethical tenets and helpful tips for aspiring principals, a riveting balance of practical case studies and sound theories of leadership. *How Expert Principals Make Difficult Decisions* is a must read for future school leaders, policy makers, and reformers."

—Bruce Fuller
Professor
University of California-Berkeley
Graduate School of Education

"In *Insights: How Expert Principals Make Difficult Decisions*, Dionne V. McLaughlin describes a sensible and cohesive approach to decision making and includes case studies of actual situations faced by real principals. McLaughlin provides useful information and guidance for busy principals who make a multitude of decisions on a daily basis. *Insights* is a valuable resource for new and aspiring principals as well as experienced principals."

—C. Diane Payne
Director, Principal Fellows Program
Center for School Leadership Development
Chapel Hill, NC

"Even as an experienced administrator, I found the book valuable in validating my own decision making during difficult situations. This book provides administrators with real stories from those working in school administration. As an administrator, I felt this book had great examples of difficult decisions, accurate steps taken to try and come to a solution, and examples of decisions made that truly make sense. I found the book to be an excellent read."

—Nicky Kemp
Assistant Superintendent
North Callaway R-1 School District
Kingdom City, MO

Insights: How Expert Principals Make Difficult Decisions

Dear Cynthia —
Glad you could come to
the session. Wish you
the best on your
dissertation.

Dionne V. McLaughlin

CORWIN
A SAGE Company

A SAGE Company

FOR INFORMATION:

Corwin

A SAGE Company

2455 Teller Road

Thousand Oaks, California 91320

(800) 233-9936

www.corwin.com

SAGE Publications Ltd.

1 Oliver's Yard

55 City Road

London EC1Y 1SP

United Kingdom

SAGE Publications India Pvt. Ltd.

B 1/I 1 Mohan Cooperative Industrial Area

Mathura Road, New Delhi 110 044

India

SAGE Publications Asia-Pacific Pte. Ltd.

3 Church Street

#10-04 Samsung Hub

Singapore 049483

Executive Editor: Arnis Burvikovs

Associate Editor: Desirée A. Bartlett

Editorial Assistant: Andrew Olson

Project Editor: Veronica Stapleton Hooper

Copy Editor: Deanna Noga

Typesetter: C&M Digitals (P) Ltd.

Proofreader: Sarah J. Duffy

Indexer: Karen Wiley

Cover Designer: Janet Kiesel

Marketing Managers: Lisa Lysne and Amy Vader

Printed in the United States of America

A catalog record of this book is available from the Library of Congress.

ISBN: 978-1-4833-5119-3

This book is printed on acid-free paper.

SUSTAINABLE FORESTRY INITIATIVE

Certified Chain of Custody
Promoting Sustainable Forestry
www.sfiprogram.org
SFI-01268

SFI label applies to text stock

15 16 17 18 19 10 9 8 7 6 5 4 3 2 1

Contents

Preface

As a new principal, I did not realize initially just how crucial decision making was to my success. I succumbed to pressure and made hasty decisions without anticipating the likely repercussions.

I wish I had been able to consult a resource like *Insights* when I was contemplating how to move my faculty toward change or when I was faced with difficult situations demanding resolution for which no decision seemed the right one. Over time, I developed a set of professional core values, but did not always make the important connection between my core values and which decisions mattered most. I also came to understand the importance of assessing school culture when making decisions to introduce change, and utilizing key problem-solving processes to resolve difficult decisions.

Homer-Dixon (2000) states,

> "We demand that (leaders) solve, or at least manage, a multitude of interconnected problems that can develop into crises without warning; we require them to navigate an increasingly turbulent reality that is, in key aspects, literally incomprehensible to the human mind; we submerge them in often unhelpful and distracting information; and we force them to decide and act at an ever faster pace" (p. 15).

One of the greatest challenges principals face is the capacity to make good decisions. As principals are bombarded with competing demands, they face the daily challenge of making a host of good decisions in a short amount of time. In this turbulent reality, principals are often obliged to make decisions with limited pertinent information. *Insights: How Expert Principals Make Difficult Decisions* is full of cases about real principals and full of the words and phrases they used to describe their own dilemmas. By conducting extensive interviews with expert principals about the difficult and complex decisions that they make on a daily basis, I have tried to tease out the factors that inform and guide those decisions. In these pages, principals speak of their core values and priorities, the cultures of their schools, the competing pressures they must withstand, and the processes they have developed to reach the best possible decisions. As the title of the book suggests, they have valuable insights to offer. With the distillation of their thoughts in this volume, I hope to provide a practical guide to strategic decision making for all principals—for new and aspiring principals as well as for those principals who are seeking to improve their decision making.

This book could be utilized for professional development for new or aspiring principals, as a supplement to a university principal preparation course, or as a guide for training principals looking for opportunities to improve their practice. Much like the professional consultation that a mentor principal can offer, *Insights* models effective decision-making processes and provides tips to guide less experienced colleagues. This book includes specific, practical leadership case studies from principals in urban and suburban settings that provide several opportunities for self-reflection. Case study resolutions and a Classroom Walkthrough instrument are included in the Resources section. Tips for making specific types of decisions are featured, for example, tips for managing a crisis with a suspected or actual weapon on school grounds, tips to consider when making policy changes, tips for managing faculty misconduct, as well as concise charts that illustrate decisions principals made to close the gap in their respective schools. Readers will be exposed to a framework for making difficult decisions in complex, unpredictable environments. Recommendations for how to avoid critical errors in decision making are also included. As an experienced bilingual high school and elementary school principal who has worked in urban and suburban settings, I also share my leadership experiences. I maintain my assertion that if school leaders are exposed to difficult and complex decisions and their resolutions, they will be better able to solve similar problems that they may encounter.

In Part I, I highlight the factors expert principals consider in decision making as well as a larger shared focus on improvement, stakeholders, and data. Strategies described include examining the whole picture, considering multiple scenarios and sifting through superfluous details, determining who else will be involved in the decision-making process, and viewing both the foreground and background of a dilemma.

In Part II of the book, I explore particular types of difficult decisions principals encountered and how they utilized strategies presented in Part I to develop a resolution. In these chapters, principals describe a wide range of decisions: for example, to conduct intense evaluations of ineffective teachers, fire a popular coach, pursue long-term suspensions, revamp a bell schedule, resolve cyberbullying, and use data to improve the performance of African American and Latino students. They shared structures they have developed in their schools, the legal implications of difficult and complex decisions, how school policy influences decision making, how to make decisions that will transform the school environment, and how to make effective decisions even in instances where trust is absent.

Introducing the Principals

The 21 principals who participated in the study—from five districts in urban and suburban counties in Massachusetts, Maryland, and North Carolina—are introduced in Table 1.0. Principals were asked the extent to which they utilized problem-solving strategies outlined in Brenninkmeyer and Spillane's (2008) framework or Davis's (2004) framework for heuristic decision making. The frameworks are utilized to examine effective decision-making practices of expert principals and to explore practical applications. Central office administrators were asked to recommend their best (expert) principals. In cases where the district expressed reluctance to name best principals, principals were selected who had been mentor principals and/or whose school's standardized test scores reflected above average school achievement for the district. Individual qualitative principal interviews (45–60 minutes) were conducted with principals in five districts in urban and suburban counties. Pseudonyms were utilized throughout. Questions were created by me in consultation with the Odum Institute and approved by my former university human rights in research committee (IRB # 2103-P-0010). The principals' administrative experience ranges from 5 to 29 years. About half the principals interviewed were female. The majority were White, but several African American and Latino principals were also interviewed. The principals led small and large schools ranging in size from 105 to 2,353 students. Principals were from traditional schools, alternative schools, and early college high schools. Some were high-poverty, majority-minority schools; several others were very prestigious, affluent schools. I enjoyed our conversations tremendously. I was amazed

Table 1.0 Expert Principals

State	Principal's Name (Pseudonym)	Race	Gender	Years of Admin. Exp.	Type of School	Socioeconomic Status (Free and reduced lunch %)	School Size
NC	Mr. Henry	White	Male	5	Urban	40%	1,268
NC	Mr. King	White	Male	13	Urban	74%	1,154
NC	Mr. Adams	White	Male	13	Urban	42%	1,195
NC	Mr. Vance	White	Male	8	Urban	100%	320
NC	Ms. Major	African American	Female	7	Urban/Early College	47%	105
NC	Mr. Edwards	White	Male	11	Urban	52%	1,725
NC	Mr. Peppers	African American	Male	29	Urban/Alternative	NR*	NR*
NC	Ms. Lyons	White	Female	12	Urban/Early College	61%	240
MD	Ms. Wallace	African American	Female	8	Urban/Alternative	81%	255
MD	Mr. Rollins	African American	Male	5	Urban	84%	326
MD	Dr. Jeffreys	African American	Female	12	Urban	89%	498
MD	Mr. Baron	White	Male	5	Urban	72%	1,659
MA	Mr. Starnes	White	Male	6	Suburban	9%	1,722
MA	Dr. Zenga	White	Female	11	Suburban	15%	1,910
MA	Ms. Cantrell	African American	Female	11	Urban	67%	320
MA	Dr. Manning	White	Female	17	Urban	30%	2,353
MA	Mr. Bliden	White	Male	4	Suburban	6%	922
MA	Ms. Rodriguez	Latina	Female	10	Urban	74%	610
MA	Ms. Perez	Latina	Female	7	Urban	55%	1,645
MA	Ms. Langely	White	Female	14	Suburban	7%	1,951
MA	Ms. Lily	White	Female	4	Urban	72%	406

*NR—Not reported

by the candor, grace, and ease with which the principals handled the extremely volatile and contentious decisions they encountered.
After reading this book, you will:

1. Discover the problem-solving strategies of expert principals, which include utilizing a data focus, improvement focus, and stakeholder focus.

2. Investigate the factors expert principals consider when making decisions to manage a crisis or make policy changes.

3. Assess the role of core values in decision making.

4. Review core values that guide principals and develop your own professional core values.

5. Ascertain the role of building trusting relationships as changes are strategically introduced.

6. Become aware of the types of decisions that can lead to regaining control of unsettling environments.

7. Articulate how school culture affects decision making.

8. Learn the practices for improving decision making using heuristic thinking.

9. Determine how examining the whole picture, expanding the field of attention, visualizing solutions, and involving others can improve decision making.

10. Adopt strategies for making difficult decisions about student disciplinary consequences.

11. Establish an Intense Teacher Evaluation Process.

12. Learn guidelines for making decisions about terminating high-profile coaches, managing duplicitous faculty practices, and dealing with allegations of faculty misconduct.

13. Review successful practices for data analysis that increase the performance of African American and Latino students.

14. Ascertain how changing structures, eliminating barriers to access, and introducing programs can increase the academic performance of African American and Latino students.

Acknowledgments

To my husband, Paul, I am deeply appreciative of your confidence and for all of your loving support during this process.

To my sons, Michael and Paul. Thank you for your understanding, your independence, your hugs, your smiles, and your encouragement.

To the 21 principals in North Carolina, Maryland, and Massachusetts. Your veracity, dedication, and temerity in the face of unexpected challenges and tremendous opposition is remarkable.

To Gail L. Thompson for introducing me to Dan and subsequently to Arnis.

To the entire team at Corwin, especially Arnis E. Burvikovs, executive editor, Desiree A. Bartlett, senior associate editor, Lisa Lysne, marketing manager, Veronica Stapleton Hooper, project editor, Deanna Noga, copy editor, Andrew Olson, editorial assistant, and Kimberly Schmidt, marketing assistant.

To Chancellor Debra Saunders-White, Dean Wynetta Lee, and Chair Laurell C. Malone for welcoming me to the North Carolina Central University family.

A special note and thanks to photographer and friend Peggy Davis. You are incredibly talented. Your patience is appreciated.

To Michelle, Linda, Tamara, Gina, Carmen, La-Eula, Johnavae, Beth, Andrea, Vanessa, Carolyn, Vivian, and Eleanor for your encouraging words, love, and support.

Publisher's Acknowledgments

Corwin would like to thank the following individuals for their editorial insight and guidance:

Dr. Virginia E. Kelsen
Principal
Rancho Cucamonga High School
Rancho Cucamonga, CA

Nicky Kemp
Assistant Superintendent
North Callaway R-1 School District
Kingdom City, MO

Dr. Noran L. Moffett and Melanie Frizzell
Associate Dean/Professor of Educational Leadership
Fayetteville State University
Fayetteville, NC

Debra Paradowski
Associate Principal
Arrowhead Union High School
Hartland, WI

Cathy Patterson
5th Grade Teacher
Walnut Valley USD
Walnut, CA

John Robinson
Principal
Newton Conover City Schools
Newton, NC

Joy Rose
High School Principal (Retired)
Westerville City Schools
Westerville, OH

About the Author

 **Dionne V. McLaughlin**, EdD, is an assistant professor in the Department of Educational Leadership at North Carolina Central University. She is a British-born Jamaican educator who is an experienced bilingual high school and elementary school principal. Dr. McLaughlin has experience as a K–12 METCO director for a voluntary desegregation program in Massachusetts and as the program director for a Latino community-based organization. Additionally, she has 11 years of teaching experience; a doctorate in educational leadership from the University of North Carolina, Chapel Hill; and a master's in education from the Harvard Graduate School of Education. Her research interests include the principalship, Blacks in Latin America, effective teachers of African American and Latino high school students, and examining the racial context of schools. Recent scholarly works include an *NCPEA* article on how administrators can improve schools by learning from the experiences of African American and Latino high school students and a *Teacher Education Journal of South Carolina* article, "The Cultural Symphony in Schools: Effectively Teaching African American and Latino High School Students." Dr. McLaughlin has also authored a chapter of a Sage book, "New South Realities, Demographics, Cultural Capital, and Diversity" in *The Sage Guide to Educational Leadership and Management* (2015). Dr. McLaughlin has led workshops for teachers, principals, and assistant principals on culturally responsive teaching, effective school practices, and making effective leadership decisions. Recent presentations include the International Conference on Urban Education (Montego Bay, Jamaica) in 2014, ASCD 2015 Conference on Teaching Excellence (Nashville, TN), and the National Association of Elementary Principals (NAESP) in 2015.

To my husband, Paul, my best friend
To my sons, Paul and Michael

PART I

Factors Expert Principals Consider in Decision Making

1

Weighing Options

Principals can become overwhelmed by mounting pressures; limited time and resources; competing demands; the needs of students, parents, and staff; and an expectation that dozens of critical decisions be made on a daily basis. Often principals feel compelled to make decisions without sufficient data, reflection, advice, or careful analysis. Making even one poor decision can cause a loss of respect and support from staff, supervisors, and parents; a series of bad decisions can trigger the voluntary or involuntary end of the principalship. Teachers and parents can be very unforgiving of bad decisions. That does not mean that principals should lead walking on eggshells, but proceeding with caution is strongly advised. Decisions, unless tied to a crisis, should be made after a period of thoughtful consideration. In this chapter, we take a look at how principals describe their own key problem-solving processes and explore two case studies in which major decisions were made, with very different results.

CASE STUDY #1

It All Started So Well—How Poorly Made Decisions Can Sabotage a Principalship

Dr. Iona was the district's top choice for principal of Coventry Oxford School. She had a master's from a top Ivy League school and a doctorate

(Continued)

(Continued)

from a nationally ranked school of education. She had 6 years of experience as a school administrator and 10 years of experience as a classroom teacher. Though most of her experience was at the high school level, she had experience as a K–12 director. Dr. Iona eagerly started her new position at Coventry Oxford School. She was warmly embraced by the faculty who had not supported her predecessor.

Within a couple of months of being at Coventry Oxford, a welcome celebration was held and teachers gave speeches about how happy they were to have Dr. Iona at their school. Dr. Iona's first priority was getting to know her teachers and being responsive to their concerns. When Dr. Iona learned that a group of teachers needed additional tutors, she scheduled a volunteer to work with students. Dr. Iona was told that communication was an issue, so she implemented several strategies to improve communication. She generated weekly **Connect Ed**, electronic mass notification messages to parents and staff, quarterly parent website messages, frequent data updates, and weekly newsletters to her staff. Dr. Iona also worked closely with her School Improvement Team and established a Leadership Team that included teachers.

Dr. Iona had an open-door policy for teachers and parents. She was responsive to parents but not intimidated by them. Even before she started her position officially, a parent sent her an e-mail requesting to change her child's teacher. Dr. Iona listened to the parent's concerns but stated both to the parent and publically to her faculty that she would not support changing teachers. The student was not moved, but the parent's concerns were addressed. Dr. Iona also did a lot of research before making decisions and followed up with teachers when parent concerns were brought to her attention. When she discovered an additional $22,000 in the budget for instructional supplies, Dr. Iona invited her teachers to give their input on how to spend the dollars. Dr. Iona was visible in classrooms and handled discipline consistently. When it became apparent that limited technology was an issue, Dr. Iona worked with the technology facilitator to obtain low-cost refurbished computers and turned a vacant classroom into an additional computer lab. Notes and requests left in Dr. Iona's mailbox were removed and addressed in a timely manner. Dr. Iona was frank and scrupulous in her dealings and sought feedback from her staff on her performance as a principal. Dr. Iona couldn't imagine working anywhere else.

Dr. Iona's second year, however, was beset with one problem after another. Though she consulted the Leadership Team and teachers about a master schedule change, the schedule she adopted created several stressors: some students ate lunch at 10:40 a.m., lunch lines were excessively long because of no breaks in the schedule, and teachers complained of being tired at the end of day because of the changes. Dr. Iona forged ahead, mistakenly thinking that the issues could be resolved given the positive gain of 75 minutes of common planning time.

Rather than inform Dr. Iona of their concerns, teachers complained to parents. Dr. Iona had developed good communication with some staff members, but she had not developed the level of trust needed to weather the storm. By the third week of school after a meeting with an influential parent and some teacher leaders, Dr. Iona realized that the scheduling concerns could not be rectified, so a move was made to return to the previous schedule with some minor changes.

In an effort to provide sufficient dollars for an intervention position, classes were scheduled at the maximum class sizes. The state changed the class size maximums, but the district did not notify principals so several classes were overcrowded at the start of the school year. A new teacher was hired to offset the overcrowding, but that resulted in students changing classes after school started.

While cleaning up this mess, Dr. Iona began to be pressured by her area superintendent to implement significant midyear changes. The required submission of professional learning community (PLC) minutes had already been introduced at the beginning of the year. Now the central office was requiring that Coventry Oxford School adopt new midyear district assessments and teachers were required to have lesson plans visible and available in classrooms during classroom walkthroughs. Teachers posted veiled concerns on a website and complained vehemently to parents about low morale. Dr. Iona felt compelled to offer teachers and parents the opportunity to share concerns in a survey that central office developed and disseminated. The results were not surprising, and the School Improvement Team and area superintendent continued to be supportive of Dr. Iona. Dr. Iona proactively anticipated the concerns and shared a plan to address concerns with parents and faculty. She also provided opportunities at Leadership Team meetings, a PTA meeting, and at faculty meetings to discuss and address concerns. Though Dr. Iona was weathering the storm, it soon became evident that it was time to consider other professional options. She was offered and accepted another administrative post, which she announced to her faculty before the end of her second year as principal.

Throughout the spring, Dr. Iona remained upbeat and responsive. She continued to work arduously and maintained several strong initiatives that she introduced during her opening-of-school faculty meeting. Dr. Iona was fortunate to leave Coventry Oxford School with her reputation intact. She proudly left her school with a significant gain on the overall composite on the state's standardized test scores.

REFLECTIVE QUESTIONS

Summarize what you know about the decisions that Dr. Iona made. What else would you like to know?

1. By all visible measures, Dr. Iona had a very successful first year. What are some of the strategies that Dr. Iona utilized that led to a successful first year?

2. What type of feedback mechanisms should Dr. Iona have put in place when she implemented the school-wide change to the master schedule?

3. What decisions should principals make about which students are allowed to change classes? How can changes to a new teacher's class be made equitably?

4. What critical errors in decision making did Dr. Iona make that eroded the trust of her faculty? What could you have done to successfully move your faculty toward the change mandated by the district?

Turn to the Resources in the back of the book for a summary of how Dr. Iona might have handled the events of her second year differently.

Key Problem-Solving Processes of Expert Principals

Expert and typical principals differ in how they would respond if faced with Dr. Iona's situation. Brenninkmeyer and Spillane (2008) distinguished between expert and typical problem-solving processes by stating that expert principals followed a plan and typical principals developed disparate solutions that were not indicative of prior planning. Expert principals, they found, utilize key problem-solving processes when faced with difficult and complex decisions. In contrast, typical principals rely on retelling negative experiences, prioritize staff needs over student needs, resort to making assumptions, focus on parent satisfaction, and emphasize outward affects, personal victories, and defeats. Experts were also described as confronting conflict, whereas typical principals eschewed conflict when dealing with problems. Findings from five studies that outlined key problem-solving processes of expert school principals are collated in Table 1.1. The problem-solving processes, though distinct, seem to fall naturally into three loosely related groups:

1. Data Focus: gathers data, analyzes the scenario, recounts relevant anecdotes, identifies and overcomes constraints, and plans approach.

2. Improvement Focus: faces conflict, considers long-term outlook, and stresses follow-up.

3. Stakeholder Focus: emphasizes student program quality, delegates, and keeps parents informed.

Table 1.1   Expert Principal Problem-Solving Processes

Data Focus	
Gathers data	Collects pertinent information as a resolution is being sought
Analyzes the scenario	Considers multiple ways problems can be framed, questions all premises and common understandings
Recounts relevant anecdotes	Makes connections to related experiences
Identifies, overcomes constraints	Develops ways of managing obstacles
Plans approach	Evidence of organized, well-planned decision making
Improvement Focus	
Faces conflicts	Sees what can be learned from conflict
Considers long-term outlook	Lasting impact of the decision on the future is an integral part of decision making
Stresses follow-up	Monitors the effect of initiatives and decisions
Stakeholder Focus	
Emphasizes student program quality	Considers the impact on student growth and learning
Delegates	Embraces shared decision making, utilizes distributed leadership style, relies on others to assist with completing tasks
Keeps parents informed	Prioritizes communicating with parents

Sources: Bullock, James, & Jamieson (1995); Chi, Glaser, & Farr (1988) as cited in Brenninkmeyer & Spillane (2008); Copland (2003); Leithwood (1995); Leithwood & Stager (1989).

In the sections that follow, each of the three broad categories of problem-solving styles is illustrated with an example drawn from my experiences as an administrator or my conversations with principals.

Data Focus

Gathering data refers to collecting pertinent information in the process of seeking a resolution. Analyzing the scenario includes considering multiple ways of framing a problem and questioning all premises and common understandings. Identifying and overcoming constraints consists of making connections to related experiences. Expert principals who plan their approach with this focus demonstrate evidence of well-planned decision making.

Ms. Edmonds: Focused on Data

Ms. Edmonds was an expert principal who made complex decisions that appeared to be made effortlessly. She invested a considerable amount of time thoughtfully contemplating her options, gathering data, and listening intently to her staff, students, and parents. In her first year as a principal at Kingston Ridge, a prestigious high school, Ms. Edmonds was confronted with a cheating scandal that rocked her community.

Ms. Edmonds had faced previous cheating issues on a much smaller scale as an administrator in a former school, but this situation was different. Ms. Edmonds spent countless hours meeting with students, teachers, parents, and her assistant principals before determining her course of action. While conducting an investigation of a student who had used a cell phone to take pictures of a test answer sheet, Ms. Edmonds uncovered another cheating issue. In the separate cheating incident, at least two students were caught on camera entering the building using an improperly secured master key. The students admitted to making copies of tests and distributing them to other students. As the investigation continued, it became apparent that 11 students were involved. Most of the students were seniors so once area colleges learned of the scandal, they asked for the names of the students who were being disciplined. Ms. Edmonds decided not to press criminal charges, but instead assigned students a zero on the tests and issued out-of-school suspensions. The consequences were in line with consequences listed in the student handbook. In her estimation, the remorse expressed by the implicated students, the rescinded college acceptances, and the peer ostracism they faced were severe enough consequences.

As the scandal unfolded, Ms. Edmonds prioritized communicating with staff electronically and she held a meeting with the entire faculty. Ms. Edmonds also sent a letter to parents and spoke candidly to the media about the incidents. Ms. Edmonds was methodical in her investigation. She gathered all the available information before moving toward a decision. She analyzed the scandal from many stakeholders' viewpoints—parents, students, faculty, central office, and outside constituents—and framed the problem in multiple ways. She treated parents and students as she would have wanted to be treated if her own child had been involved in a scandal of this magnitude. Her care for students, parents, and her faculty was evident in how she handled the situation. She carefully weighed the possible consequences of student criminal charges, the impact of student academic consequences, the need to secure the building given the distribution of the master keys, teacher sentiments, parental responses, media attention, and the reputation and culture of the school. Ms. Edmonds faced the conflict and used a well-planned approach that allowed her school to frame the scandal as a learning experience. In short, Ms. Edmonds focused on data in her decision making.

Improvement Focus

Facing conflict consists of seeing what can be learned from conflict. Considering the long-term outlook includes examining the lasting impact of the decision on the future. Focusing on following up refers to monitoring the effect of initiatives and decisions.

Ms. Steadman: Focused on Improvement

Ms. Steadman, the principal of Morant Surrey High School, had 7 years' experience supervising and evaluating teachers. During that time, she had hired, supervised, and recommended underperforming teachers for nonrenewal. Ms. Wilmington was a nontenured French teacher who had been working at Morant Surrey High School for 2 years when Ms. Steadman arrived. Ms. Wilmington seemed to have a good command of the spoken and written language. Initial observations revealed that Ms. Wilmington was prepared for class and that her students were engaged and on task. She introduced grammar games and humor and connected with her student athletes.

While conducting classroom walkthroughs and observations, several concerns became evident. Ms. Steadman decided to increase her monitoring of Ms. Wilmington's performance and required Ms. Wilmington to submit district-mandated curriculum guides for all courses she was teaching, a detailed syllabus, an assessment calendar, and a plan for improving the performance of French students. Ms. Steadman documented in a midyear evaluation that Ms. Wilmington did not provide any of the requested information. Ms. Steadman also noted that a male student in Ms. Wilmington's class was wearing headphones during the introduction of a new grammar concept. Ms. Wilmington was encouraged to interrupt such behavior if it were to occur again. While Ms. Wilmington may have needed to teach some grammatical concepts in English, she was advised to use more of the target language for instruction. Ms. Wilmington was also told to attend a school-funded Advanced Placement (AP) French workshop, but she failed to attend.

During Ms. Wilmington's initial tenure at Morant Surrey High School, she gave all appearances of being a dedicated French language teacher but soon her attendance began to slip, marital issues with her spouse developed, and complaints from students and parents began to surface. A French parent contacted the principal and expressed concerns about Ms. Wilmington's ability to adequately prepare students for the AP French exam. Students also complained that Ms. Wilmington talked incessantly with them about her marital problems. It soon became evident that Ms. Wilmington was not meeting expectations and Ms. Steadman needed to make a decision. On midyear and end-of-year teacher performance reviews, several recommendations were listed. Ms. Wilmington's attendance became a concern. During the first 3 months of the school year, Ms. Wilmington had already missed 10 days. When she was absent, lesson plans were inadequate or nonexistent. For one absence, Ms. Wilmington left an English video with French subtitles, which students said they had already watched multiple times. Though a native speaker was available as a substitute, Ms. Wilmington refused to contact the sub citing concerns about the sub's adherence to her lesson plans.

At the conclusion of the second year of closely supervising Ms. Wilmington, Ms. Steadman made the decision not to recommend Ms. Wilmington for continued employment as a teacher at Morant Surrey High School. Though Ms. Steadman spent an inordinate amount of time conducting observations, meeting with Ms. Wilmington, and writing evaluations, it was worth it to ensure that her students received quality instruction. Ms. Steadman decided to face the conflict introduced by an underperforming teacher, consider the long-term impact of taking the steps necessary to remove the teacher, and follow up repeatedly on her recommendations with written feedback. Ms. Steadman made decisions that illustrated her focus on improving instruction.

Stakeholder Focus

Focusing on student program quality includes considering the impact on student growth and learning. Delegating includes utilizing shared decision making and distributed leadership. Keeping parents informed includes prioritizing regular communication with parents.

Principal Lee: Focused on Stakeholders

Principal Lee considered the decisions that she would need to make to improve the performance of rising ninth graders on the End of Course (EOC) tests at Manchester Key High School. Manchester Key had a rising ninth-grade class of 350 students. Of the 17 ninth-grade students who did not pass the EOC, eight were English Language Learners (ELLs), nine were African American, and only one was White. Ms. Lee reviewed the students' transcripts and found that only half the students were enrolled in Reading and their eighth-grade End of Grade (EOG) test scores ranged from 44% to 39%. She shared her assessment with the English department chair, Ms. Ogden. Ms. Lee concluded that they needed to create targeted English as a Second Language (ESL) support and a well-developed program to prepare students for ninth-grade English, enroll students who earned 1s and 2s (failing marks) on the EOGs in a ninth-grade Reading class, and avoid the predictability of race: that is, of having African American and Latino students constitute the majority of students failing to pass the English I EOC (all except three were Asian). Ms. Lee talked with the department chair, Ms. Ogden, about how the English department, ESL department, Reading teacher, and school administration could work together to help ESL students and African American students with 1s or 2s on the eighth-grade Reading EOG be successful in ninth-grade English.

The vacant ESL coordinator position was filled by Dr. Garvey. After inheriting a department that was ill-functioning at best, Dr. Garvey reinvigorated relationships with faculty and articulated strategies for collaboration with teachers to serve the needs of ELLs. Dr. Garvey became well versed in the curriculum of the classes her students were taking. During scheduled study sessions, Dr. Garvey used scaffolding to reteach difficult concepts and to ensure her students' success. She defined academic vocabulary, highlighted nuances in the English language, and prepared study guides. Dr. Garvey was available to students during lunch and after school and assisted students with navigating local outside agencies. Principal Lee and Ms. Ogden also concluded that another strategy would be to require all entering ninth graders to take Reading. One obstacle they encountered was that high school students were embarrassed to have Reading listed on their schedule or transcript. Principal Lee consulted with the assistant superintendent, Reading teachers in other schools, and other principals about renaming the course. After several e-mails and meetings, the course was renamed EOC Preparation.

After consulting with the middle school, a letter was sent to all rising ninth graders in the summer who failed the eighth-grade Reading EOG. The letter informed parents that their child would be required to be enrolled in a reading class—EOC Preparation. Principal Lee and the department chair consistently supported the decision that no students would be allowed to drop the course. The Reading teacher helped develop the language for the letter and followed up personally with all the families. The letter stated that students would be screened and placed in the appropriate level using the Scholastic Reading Inventory (SRI). The goal was to improve reading skills and for students to practice reading texts that were of high interest and matched their reading levels. At the end of the first semester, those students reading on grade level would be allowed to drop the class. The communication with parents emphasized the expectation that all students show significant growth and successfully pass their EOCs. Ms. Lee made critical decisions that resulted in a successful instructional effort to improve the achievement of her lowest performing students. She collaborated with teachers and coordinators in her building and administrators across the district and maintained communication with parents regarding her efforts. In short, Ms. Lee focused on the stakeholders at her school.

CASE STUDY #2

Effectively Addressing an Egregious Error

Ms. Steadman, the principal of Morant Surrey High School, a college preparatory high school, customarily spent the days at the close of the school year reviewing reports on the number of students who had earned Ds and Fs as final grades. This year, she decided to take a closer look. In addition to tallying percentages and noting familiar names, she decided to look at some of the transcripts of students with two or more Fs. After reviewing the transcripts, she made a shocking discovery. She found dozens of glaring errors. Students were not enrolled in the correct sequence of courses needed for graduation, students were reenrolled in courses that they had already passed, and students who had failed a prerequisite course were then enrolled in an Honors course. Roberto, a male Latino student in his fifth year of high school, had taken Algebra I 4 years in a row. Another Latino male student, Juan Jose, in his sixth year in high school, took World History as a ninth grader, got an A, repeated tenth grade, enrolled in World History again, earned a D, then took World History a third time and earned a C. Beatriz, a Latina female student, took English I, earned an F for the year, and then she was enrolled in Honors English I. An African American male student, Marvin, was a third-year ninth grader who was not enrolled in any math classes. Although math is a 4-year requirement, Marvin did not have math at all his second year in high school. Marvin was enrolled in U.S. History (eleventh-grade course) before Civics and Economics (tenth-grade course) and English IV before passing English III.

Ms. Steadman carefully analyzed her findings then developed a plan to share the data with the counseling department. She initially shared the data with two of the counselors whose students had errors on their transcripts and met with the Guidance department chair. They were appalled and also embarrassed by the errors. At the Guidance meeting with the other counselors, Ms. Steadman began by telling counselors that she believed that they had an effective counseling team that was working hard to support students. She expressed concerns that the students who were receiving most of their attention were the students applying to Ivy League schools and other highly selective schools. Because of the volume of parent e-mail, meetings, and phone calls, and the parents' diligence in following their children's courses, it would be highly unlikely that the children of their most affluent parents would have errors on their transcripts. Given this, Ms. Steadman indicated that she wanted to make sure that adequate time was spent reviewing the transcripts of their most fragile students.

Before presenting specific errors, Ms. Steadman acknowledged that at the request of counselors, there had been significant structural changes in the counseling department. The changes included adjustments in the grade levels assigned to counselors and a switch in the groups of students assigned alphabetically, for which counselors were responsible. Ms. Steadman also mentioned that there had been a lot of transition in the ESL department as well so some of the scheduling and transcript concerns might otherwise have been caught. In the next portion of the meeting, Ms. Steadman presented her discovery to counselors and introduced a plan to immediately address the flagrant errors. Ms. Steadman also solicited feedback on how to ensure that the errors did not reoccur.

REFLECTIVE QUESTIONS

Develop a summary of what you know about what happened. What else would you like to know?

1. Ms. Steadman outlined the process that she followed to communicate with individual counselors, the department chair, and the counseling team. How would you present the transcript errors to the counseling team?

2. How would you counter the assertion that counselors had insufficient time to carefully review all student transcripts in their caseload?

3. Would consequences be assigned to counselors who were responsible for the errors? Why or why not?

4. Given that the majority of transcript errors involved minority students, English Language Learners, and other fragile learners, what systems would you put in place to ensure that these transcript errors did not resurface?

5. What type of communication with parents and students would you initiate?

Turn to the Resources in the back of the book for a summary of how Ms. Steadman managed this situation.

Summary

There were clear warning signs that Dr. Iona overlooked that signaled that she was headed for trouble. Dr. Iona missed an opportunity to build on the success of her first year and instead spent her second year rebuilding her school community and salvaging her career.

Although Dr. Iona gathered data, attempted to analyze the scenarios, and faced the conflicts, she did not have a repertoire of experiences that would have allowed her to recount relevant anecdotes. Many of the decisions she faced were new to her so she just muddled her way through each situation. She used faulty reasoning to identify the constraints so the long-term outlook was therefore inaccurate. She did not utilize district resources and supports that could have helped her successfully manage her decisions. She focused on student program quality, but her analysis and the solutions developed were flawed (Brenninkmeyer & Spillane, 2008). Dr. Iona could have avoided potential pitfalls by learning from the experiences of expert principals and developing a schema for making effective decisions.

On the other hand, Ms. Steadman used the problem-solving processes of an expert principal. Her schema for effective decision making included making the achievement of her most fragile students her priority. She gathered data and, after analyzing the scenario, made a decision to confront her counselors when egregious errors were detected. Ms. Steadman also recognized that blaming or embarrassing her counselors would be counterproductive. It was more important to acknowledge the errors, make a plan of improvement, and ensure she followed up. Ms. Steadman focused on program quality, dealt directly with the problem, and worked with counselors to develop a well-planned approach to the problem they faced.

In the following chapters, we see how 21 expert principals describe engaging in the key problem-solving practices outlined above when confronted with difficult and complex decisions. Additionally, principals relay how their core values, the school's culture, the impact of their decisions on faculty and students, the scope of the decision, and feedback from others affected their decision making.

2

Recognizing and Connecting to Core Values

Whenever I make decisions, if it is something about my core values,
I will make that decision even if I have to expend political capital
and take the heat.

Dr. Zenga, Principal—Massachusetts

This chapter is the first of three chapters in Part I of this book in which I explore the major factors that expert principals consider in their decision making: their own core values, the school's culture, and the impact of difficult decisions on faculty and staff. Before discussing what the interviewed principals had to say, let me share some of my own experience, as a way to illustrate what I mean by core values. Bear in mind that there is no right set of values, and that equally effective principals may hold quite different beliefs and perspectives. But I do believe it is important to identify your own core values in order to be effective as a school leader and to weigh your decisions with those values in mind. I define **core values** as fundamental beliefs or guiding principles that influence behavior. Over the course of my career as a principal, I have developed the following five guidelines that spring from my core values and that I consider when making decisions.

My Leadership Core Values

1. Keep relationships central: Consider the impact of decisions on the people around you. Who will be impacted and how?

2. Take the time to carefully consider decisions. Do not rush unless there is truly an immediate crisis.

3. Be as forgiving of teachers as you are of students.

4. Always keep students' best interests in mind.

5. Be fair, consistent, and compassionate.

Keep Relationships Central

Part of the role of school leaders is to make sure that teachers feel cared for and respected. When I make decisions, I believe it is important to recognize that teachers can become uncomfortable and that I should be willing to confront teachers in a way that keeps the relationship central. While it is true that as a principal, I am a school leader, ultimately, I am leading people—and the human impact should always be the primary consideration when I am making decisions.

Take the Time to Carefully Consider Decisions

As a new school leader, it is easy to misjudge the critical nature of certain decisions. I try to carefully consider all options to prevent a small problem from snowballing into a series of bigger problems. Each decision should be given careful consideration. You will encounter many types of decisions, including decisions about school policy, programs, student achievement, teacher performance, and discipline. I find it helpful to treat decision making as if I have just been selected to appear on a new reality show, "Real Principals," and my every move is being monitored. This imagined scenario has the effect of making me slow down. Unless there is a true crisis, I think it is important to take your time, to think about your options overnight, and to treat the decision carefully. Teachers can be incredibly unforgiving of bad decisions. One bad decision could cause you to lose respect or support.

Be as Forgiving of Teachers as You Are of Students

As a school leader, your staff are your classroom. I have found it important to be aware of whom I can trust, but to treat even the most untrustworthy staff member respectfully. In spite of the fact that a faculty member may have taken an opportunity to question my authority, I find it is counterproductive to be vindictive: for example, to use the teacher evaluation instrument or my control of the master schedule to punish teachers who have treated me poorly. It is best to forgive them for their bad behavior and move on. I believe a principal's focus should be on moving out ineffective teachers and supporting effective ones. We should not feel threatened by teachers who are opinionated and outspoken and who think differently than we do, and we should not use those characteristics as a measure of their effectiveness as teachers.

Always Keep Students' Best Interests in Mind

The driving force behind every decision should be its potential impact on students: Will its overall effect be beneficial or harmful? Once, I had a very outspoken, well-respected tenured teacher on my staff who was going to be out of town on the date we had set for a year-end field trip. It was either reschedule the field trip or have students take the end-of-course retest after they returned from the field trip so she would be able to chaperone. I made the poor decision to schedule the retest based on the teacher's availability. It was not in the students' best interest to schedule an end-of-course retest after returning from an out-of-state field trip. The benefit of taking the retest immediately following remediation was lost. While we should attempt to accommodate teacher requests whenever possible, that should not be done at the expense of students. In subsequent years, I made the decision to always choose the needs of students first over those of teachers. Students should be a principal's priority.

Be Fair, Consistent, and Compassionate

In matters of discipline, a principal needs to walk a fine line: between, on the one hand, assigning consequences in a prescriptive, rote way, without any consideration of the circumstances and, on the other hand, allowing knowledge of students or their parents to unduly affect decisions. In my third year as an assistant principal, I was faced with the challenge of disciplining five ninth graders who had been harassing another ninth grader on the bus. They thought that the boy was gay so they made some vulgar gestures and attacked the boy physically as

(Continued)

(Continued)

well. The boys were all my neighbors. One of the boys was the brother of a boy who was good friends with my son. I did not assign consequences based on whether we were neighbors or friends. I treated the boys the way I would have wanted them to be treated if my son had been the victim of such an attack. The boys were suspended according to school policy, but I handled the incident with a lot of care. I was compassionate as I assigned the consequences and made sure the boys and families knew that they would not be eyed suspiciously from that point forward. I did not, however, give any leniency regarding consequences. I also provided support to the boy who was the victim of the attacks and followed up to make sure there were no further incidents.

Since I believe in being fair when assigning disciplinary consequences, I review the student handbook to ensure that consequences for violations match school and district policy. To address those violations not explicitly outlined in the handbook, I keep a copy of the handbook in which I record the consequences I assigned for a particular offense. When another student commits the same offense, I refer to my notes recorded in the handbook then that student is given the same consequence. Although we are sometimes forced to issue harsh consequences for poor student choices, I assign those consequences compassionately, not equating the student with the behavior nor repeatedly reminding the student of his or her offense.

REFLECTIVE QUESTION

Examine your core values. Write your answer to the following question: What are three or four core values that determine how you make decisions?

How Core Values Guide Principals' Decisions

What is important to note about core values is not so much their content, but rather the effect core values have on the manner in which principals make decisions. The principals I interviewed in Maryland, Massachusetts, and North Carolina described the impact that core values have on their decision making, and their responses had some common themes. Principals were asked what factors they consider when making decisions and whether or not they have any specific guiding principles. In our interviews, the terms *guiding principles* and *core values* are used interchangeably.

The principals reported that their core values have an influence on whether they do the following:

- are willing to make controversial decisions
- allow morality and ethics to guide decision making
- connect decisions to the school mission
- ground decisions in law
- remain steady and calm when making decisions
- make decisions in the best interest of students
- practice transparency in decision making and value transparency in others
- own everything that happens in the building
- spend sufficient time on decision making

Dufresne and McKenzie (2009) report that ethical leaders align actions with beliefs that emanate from core values. In some cases, the principal's core values are listed here, but the primary focus is on how the core values influenced decision making. Rather than making decisions apart from their core values, expert principals developed professional core values then consciously made decisions that emanated from those core values.

Are Willing to Make Controversial Decisions

Principal Zenga (MA) stated that her core values are equal access to an excellent education with a clear understanding that equal does not mean the same. Dr. Zenga added that if she is making a decision that does not involve these core values, she will make a decision that is politically expedient. If the decision is connected to her core values, however, she willingly makes controversial decisions even if others disagree with her decision. Additionally, Dr. Zenga prioritizes working with her faculty on issues related to class, race, and achievement. Dr. Zenga made the decision to eliminate her school's practice of only offering financial assistance for field trips to her economically disadvantaged students. Financial assistance was offered to all so that economically disadvantaged students would not be singled out. Decisions that benefit racial minorities or economically disadvantaged students can be controversial. The principal's core values should drive decision making and determine whether a particular decision merits engagement in controversy with faculty, students, or parents. Decisions unconnected to core values can be delegated and made by other capable members of the school community.

Principal Baron (MD) mentioned, "Every decision I make, I believe in the 80/20 rule. Twenty percent of all my decisions matter, 80% do not. I have to know what is important to me and if it's going into my 20%." Building trusting relationships with students is one of Mr. Baron's core values. Principal Baron makes professional development decisions connected to his core values. He obtained funds to send the entire staff of his small 350-student school to Texas to attend the Capturing Kids' Hearts training. Mr. Baron considered this investment critical to building the relational capacity of his teachers. While taking staff to Texas may not be controversial, the use of funding could be. Mr. Baron had to be willing to justify the professional development expense of thousands of dollars and to explain to his school community why such an expense was legitimate. Decisions about how a principal spends money can be controversial. Both Dr. Zenga and Mr. Baron are willing to make controversial decisions based on what they value if the decisions are connected to their core values. Conversely, if a decision involves no connection to core values, the principal might consider delegating the decision to a staff member.

Allow Morality and Ethics to Guide Decision Making

Principals also expressed a willingness to make controversial decisions if those decisions were based on moral or ethical principles. Mr. Adams (NC) stated that his moral and ethical values guide his decision making and added, "You have to do what is in the best interest of your stakeholders, but at the same time, you can't allow them to have you make an immoral decision. Sometimes the best decision is not the most popular." Mr. Adams always remembers that he has a building of 1,100 students and he has to make decisions in the best interest of all of them. The right decision, he believes, takes precedence over expediency, loyalty, and convenience. Acting morally and ethically can be unpopular, but morality must come before pleasing a powerful parent or star student athlete. Student consequences need to be the same regardless of the child's parent, age, or the family's role in the community. Mr. Adams acknowledged that when he faced a decision that was contrary to his ethical beliefs or values he willingly made the right decision regardless of whether it was difficult, controversial, time consuming, or inconvenient.

When I worked as an administrator in an affluent suburban district, I had to make a decision about suspending a star basketball player. He instigated a fight between two students that took place in the cafeteria. I assigned a consequence based on his offense. I suspended the student for 3 days. Based on when the offense took place, his suspension affected his ability to play in a basketball game. I did not change the dates of the suspension to accommodate his ability to play. In my estimation, it would have been unethical to change the dates of the suspension or end the suspension prematurely. My core values about being fair and consistent and my beliefs about what is ethical influenced my decision about issuing a student consequence.

The principal's professional core values should be an essential component of decision making. Ms. Major (NC) expressed that she tries to be fair and consistent, open minded, and nonjudgmental, and she tries to consider all the potential ramifications of her decisions. Ms. Major puts herself in the role of the devil's advocate and anticipates opposing viewpoints. Ms. Major concluded, "The guiding principles differ depending on what the decision may be—being ethical, fair, and consistent are what I try to keep in the forefront of my mind." Principal Jeffreys (MD) ascertains the morality and legality of her decision and whether her decision will be perceived by others as intended. "I look at the situation before me. If it's not illegal, immoral, or unethical, how do I couch the response so that people can receive the decision the way I intend for it?" Dr. Jeffreys's description of her decision-making process is consistent with engaging in reflective equilibrium, that is, the practice on deliberating about moral convictions, adapting beliefs, and determining ethical principles that drive decisions (Pauken, 2012).

Connect Decisions to the School Mission

Principals also stated that their decisions were influenced by the mission of their school. Principal Jeffreys (MD) asserted that she thinks about the mission and vision of the school when she is making decisions. She asks herself and her staff if the direction they are about to take is consistent with what their mission or vision says they are going to do. Principal Rollins (MD) concurred, "The vision and the mission statement—what we say we're about. Knowing what your initiatives are for the year. Keeping those things in front of you helps with the decision making." Mr. Rollins keeps his staff focused on what they should be doing for students. He admits that this does not cover every situation, but he adds that it keeps him focused and prevents him from moving in too many different directions. The principal's articulated core values should be in concert with the school's core values, and decisions made should be reflective of those core values.

> "I try to hold to the core values of the school." Principal Perez (MA)

As Ms. Lily (MA) is making a decision, she is influenced by how the decision contributes to building the community of faculty or assists in clarifying the mission and learning philosophy of the school. Ms. Perez (MA) mentioned, "I try to hold to the core values of the school and make sure that my decisions are the best that I can do for the students here." Ms. Perez focuses on making decisions related to her school's core values. While in most cases, principals made decisions in conjunction with their school's mission and core values, Ms. Rodriguez (MA) countered, "The school's (core values) are totally against my philosophy. When I do something, I keep in mind that they don't have the same mindset, framework." Ms. Rodriguez had a 2-year assignment to turn around a struggling urban school in her district, so she was faced with many teachers with opposing viewpoints and others who had been engaged in behavior that was not in the best interest of students. The school was functioning according to a set of core values that were the antithesis of those being advocated for by Ms. Rodriguez. In this case, the school leader was purposely making decisions contrary to rather than in accordance with the school's core values.

Ground Decisions in Law

In addition to being willing to make controversial decisions, making moral and ethical decisions, and connecting decisions to the school mission, principals shared that their core values affected their attention to policy and law, especially in the presence of immoral, illegal, or unethical alternatives. As Mattocks (2006) so aptly described it, educational leadership takes place under "a giant umbrella of laws, rules, and regulations" (p. 105). Principals readily acknowledged that they made decisions based on adherence to policy and law. That is not a given. In 2013, 35 Atlanta principals and teachers were indicted for making unprincipled decisions to provide students with answers, change student answers on the CRCT (Criterion-Referenced Competency Test), or repress whistle-blowers (Winerip, 2013). Rather than looking at ways to skirt the law or ignore district policy, principals shared that they valued law and policy and considered law and policy integral parts of their decision making.

> "What is legal, won't cost my job, won't send me to jail?" Principal Jeffreys (MD)

After noting significant issues with tardies and attendance at my new school, I felt compelled to implement a more stringent tardy policy. My area superintendent encouraged me to ground my decision in **school board** policy and work in conjunction with the school improvement team. I researched school board policy on attendance and tardies then presented my proposal to the school improvement team. A new school policy was adopted that adhered to law and district school board policy.

Principal Jeffreys (MD) stated, "The first thing when I make a decision: What is legal, won't cost my job, won't send me to jail? What led up to it and what's the long-term effect? If I do this, how will it be perceived so it doesn't cause more problems later?" Principal Jeffreys reviews the legal parameters as well as other factors when she is making a decision. Some decisions are very straightforward. If law or policy could be violated, another option should be considered.

Ms. Lyons (NC) indicated, "If it is policy that is law. We are going to follow policy. If it is in the guidelines, what is best for students? That is what we are here for." Ms. Lyons investigates the legal and school board policy related to her decisions and makes sure that she adheres to policy. She also considers how the policy affects her students. Ms. Major (NC) highlighted the importance of gathering information from an investigation and following guidelines and procedures established by the school system. It is important for principals to be knowledgeable about school policy. The principal's ensuing actions, assigned consequences, and priorities need to line up with school board/**school committee** policy and law. Checking school board/school committee policy helps principals identify the boundaries of their legal authority in decision making.

Remain Steady and Calm When Making Decisions

Other factors that influenced how core values impacted decision making included remaining calm in emotionally charged environments and prioritizing students by making decisions in the best interest of students. Mr. Adams (NC) prioritizes being calm when making decisions in emotionally charged environments. When he feels he is getting upset, he has put in place a protocol that helps him regain his composure. Mr. Adams stated, "I never allow my staff to ever see me lose my cool. If I get upset, I call my secretary and tell her that I'm going to make sure Mr. Gillis (fictitious person) has mowed the lawn and she knows I need a moment." In the busy day of a principal, it is

"I never allow my staff to ever see me lose my cool." Principal Adams (NC)

hard to find time to go the bathroom, eat lunch, or take an unscheduled break. It can be invaluable, however, to step away from an emotionally charged situation to gain some much-needed perspective before forging ahead with a decision that could be detrimental.

Make Decisions in the Best Interest of Students

Core values determined what principals prioritized. Of the 21 principals interviewed, 14 mentioned that they prioritize the best interest of students when making decisions. Mr. Starnes (MA) added, "What goes through my mind is what is best for kids? That is what it comes down to. That is what we are here for." Mr. Bliden (MA) stated that he is a fairly practical and pragmatic person. He considers whatever has the greatest benefit for the greatest amount of students. He does not focus on the way things have been done in the past. Referring to a staffing decision, Mr. Bliden added that he recently made the decision to nonrenew a nontenured teacher. He shared that he considers what he would do if his daughter was in that class. The decision was

"The number one thing is what is best for the students." Ms. Perez (MA)

not a hard decision because it was the right decision, but breaking the news was difficult. It is not in the best interest of students to retain an underperforming teacher who has been given

opportunities and support to improve but is not making adequate progress.

Principals should anticipate how their decisions will impact students. Ms. Perez stressed, "The number one thing is what is best for the students, then after that what will be best for teachers to maximize learning, then what is best for administrators to best help teachers and is everyone aligned with maximizing learning?" Ms. Perez makes sure that as she is making decisions, the decisions do not interfere with instructional time. When students are the priority, decision-making options are narrowed and focused.

Practice Transparency in Decision Making and Value Transparency in Others

Their core values determined whether principals engaged in transparency in decision making. Ms. Lily (MA) recounted her experience with

a weapon on campus in her urban high school and the subsequent decisions she made. "Earlier in the year, a gun was brought into the school.
I tend to bring the staff together and process that. My style is living in
transparency and trying to take the human element into consideration."
Ms. Lily values openness in her decision making. She anticipated her
faculty would want answers about
the incident so she brought them
together for a faculty meeting and
provided her teachers with relevant information and a forum for
teachers to discuss their concerns.

> "Be direct. Be honest. Whether the person
> agrees or not, at least they know why."
> Mr. Vance (NC)

Mr. Vance also practices transparency in his decision making, saying, "I want to be direct and not beat around the bush. This is why the
decision is being made. Qualify the rationale or the decision. Be direct.
Be honest. Whether the person agrees or not, at least they know why."
Each principal should determine how the core values they ascribe to
will ultimately affect their decision making. Transparency can bring
a higher level of scrutiny from faculty and parents, but the absence
of transparency can lead to criticism about a lack of inclusion in decision making. Principals have to sort through the difference between
transparency and confidentiality. Some aspects of decision making,
particularly those pertaining to personnel matters or student privacy,
simply cannot be shared.

Principals also communicated about their expectation that members of their staff would be open in their communication. This type of
transparency cannot be forced and may only develop over time with
a group of trusted teachers. Mr. Starnes (MA) divulged that he makes
it a goal to not be the smartest person in the room. He values truth
and relies on the opinions of others. He wants all the information
when he is making a decision and he encourages staff to be frank,
even if the information they share is hard to hear. He has a quote on
his wall from Gandhi that illustrates this core value: "Even if you are
the minority of one, the truth is still the truth." Principals can expect
transparency and even nurture transparency, but it should never be
demanded. Genuine transparency from staff can help principals
make better decisions.

Own Everything That Happens in the Building

Another core value that influences decision making is the belief that
principals are ultimately responsible for everything that takes place
in their school, the good and the bad. Therefore when teachers or

students succeed, the principal succeeds, but when they do not, the principal shoulders that burden as well. There is an identification with and support for those teachers and students that are part of the school family. Principal Rollins (MD) asserted that when he is talking about his students or his teachers, he is talking about himself. If his students are failing high-stakes assessments, he asks what he can do better to help his teachers help the students or improve how teachers talk to parents. As an example, Mr. Rollins shared, "It could be something as simple as a teacher missed a deadline. What did I do to allow that to happen? Did I give them the information?" Mr. Rollins mentioned that he has some extreme cases where he did not have anything to do with the result, but he is slow to point fingers. It is vital to make decisions influenced by professional core values that prioritize your ownership of what takes place in your building, particularly when things do not go well.

Spend Sufficient Time on Decision Making

Nearly every principal noted his or her beliefs about the importance of investing sufficient time in making the best possible decision and of judging the relative urgency of different kinds of decisions. Sometimes it is not necessary to have a significant amount of time to make decisions, but the planning needed to implement the decision takes time.

There may not be a lot of turnaround time for a personnel decision or for a decision about a student disciplinary consequence. Sometimes decisions are made in a split second; in other cases principals have time to think about the decision. It depends on the situation and the nature of the decision. Principal Rollins (MD) expressed, "Budget season—I was given a month for a budget. Sometimes there's a parent complaint and I need an answer in 2 hours." Ideally there is 24 to 48 hours to think and consider the decision and get feedback as appropriate from affected stakeholders. Ms. Lyons (NC) tries to do her research before making a decision unless it is an emergency. How much time does she take to make a decision? "It depends. Some decisions you can make instantly. I never make a decision about discipline instantly because I like to have a student reflect on their decisions.

> "What happens is we react in a nanosecond. That is when we make mistakes." Ms. Langely (MA)

Unless it is an emergency, a 911, then it's an instant decision." If decisions are not made thoughtfully, mistakes can be made. To avoid that, the outcomes of the decision need to be considered. Ms. Langely said, "Take the time that is needed to make the decision. What happens is we react in a nanosecond. That is when we make mistakes. Make sure we have gone through why we think that is the right decision. What are the positive outcomes?" Ms. Langely added that the majority of people want decisions in 5 minutes, and because she has so much history with the school, she can make decisions related to day-to-day operations fairly quickly. She spends days on decisions related to people. Principal Rollins (MD) concurred then added, "I make my best decisions when I have time to align them with my beliefs."

Summary

While ethics may not change, as principals progress in their careers, some core values may evolve. Core values may emanate from a distillation of experiences as well as personal inclinations or predispositions toward a certain set of behaviors. This chapter explored how core values shape principals' decision making. Principals develop their own professional core values, which are intricately connected to their leadership decisions. Core values influenced whether a principal is willing to make controversial decisions. Dr. Zenga (MA) asserted that her decisions go into two camps. Sometimes she has to make decisions and does not know what camp it falls into. Is it about her core values or is it not? Around her core values, she will make less popular decisions and around her non–core values, she will make the politically expedient decisions. Principals also shared that their core values guided their decision making when faced with immoral, illegal, or unethical options. Transparency in decision making was valued, in that principals were forthright and open about their decision-making practices. Core values also impacted how time was utilized in decision making and helped determine priorities.

3

Considering the Culture Before Introducing Change

The thing about this place. There is so much history.
As we go through the year, tradition runs this school.

Mr. Henry, Principal—North Carolina

To make effective decisions as a principal, it is critical to become a student of your environment. For principals of a large school, like Mr. Henry's (NC) that is infused with tradition, those traditions that are part of the school's culture should be an integral part of decision making. Learning about the culture of a school requires discrete observation, attention to detail, and the ability to accurately assess organizational culture. Connolly, James, and Beales (2011) advocate for understanding "different perspectives about organizational culture—external reality, interpretation, organization, competing subcultures, and process" (p. 422). These perspectives suggest that culture can be viewed as a reality outside of the individual; as symbols, shared beliefs, or values that must be interpreted to be understood; as an organization inextricably linked with culture; or as a mixture of opposing subcultures.

There is no substitute for becoming intimately acquainted with the data, history, and demographics of your school. This chapter explores the value of getting to know the school's culture to make good decisions and effectively introduce change.

First, Consider the Culture: A Cautionary Tale

Some years ago when I working as a principal in Massachusetts at an urban high school, I was confronted with my students' below average performance on MCAS (the Massachusetts Comprehensive Assessment System), a statewide standardized test developed to assess students' mastery of the state curriculum frameworks. In seeking to find ways to improve their performance, I introduced the idea of having teachers and administrators take the MCAS. I floated the idea by a few trusted teachers who told me what I wanted to hear and led me to believe that it was a worthwhile endeavor. Within a very short period of time, however, it became evident that teachers in my building were extremely resistant to the plan. One teacher and union representative, Ms. Beavers, met with me to discuss her concerns and the concerns of the faculty. She expressed reluctance about taking the exam and questioned how the results would be utilized. She helped me see the angst that had been created by this idea and assured me that this did not in any way reflect the faculty's commitment to student achievement. Teachers were understandably reticent about being required to take the MCAS. Information had not been clearly communicated about what would be done with the results and many likely questioned whether they themselves would do well on the assessment.

I considered the cost of fracturing the faculty and the ensuing backlash if I proceeded. Ultimately, I recanted and found another, less controversial way of achieving the same results—I formulated an alternative that included fruitful dialogue about **test item deconstruction** with the faculty in small department meetings. Test item deconstruction (an approach to curriculum alignment) begins with "publically released test items and deconstruct(s) (break(s) them into smaller analytical pieces) to discern the level of cognitive ability, the format and the type of content" (English, 2006, p. 42). I had not yet developed trusting relationships with my entire faculty so that they would understand that the intent of the initiative was learning about the MCAS assessment, not inquiring about their ability. Thus, my attempt to introduce change was unsuccessful; I had not accurately assessed the culture in my school and the potential impact that such a change would have on the environment in the school community. Had I learned more about the culture in my building, I would have realized that the school had recently experienced an extremely unpopular restructuring from a larger high school into three separate small schools. The ensuing changes had divided the faculty, and the top-down manner in which the changes were imposed left many faculty members bitter and distrustful. When I arrived, the school was in its first year of existence as a new small school, so changes needed to be carefully and thoughtfully introduced. A great deal of time was needed for healing and building a cohesive, healthy climate.

Tips for Measuring School Climate

1. Observation

2. Interviews and meetings

3. Town hall discussions

4. Study circles and focus groups

Source: Cohen, Pickeral, & McCloskey (2008/2009).

After careful observation of faculty behavior, reflection, and discussions with members of my faculty and central office about the history and context of my school, I was better able to understand my school's culture.

As I pondered future decisions, I was able to ascertain the impact that school culture would have on my decisions as a principal. This chapter examines the context of culture and its effect on the decision making of principals.

Effecting Change in Different School Cultures

To illustrate what the interviewed principals had learned about their school cultures and how those different cultures affected their decisions and the introduction of change, the experiences of four principals are portrayed here. Two principals of high-profile, traditional schools reveal the challenges of making decisions in highly scrutinized environments. Two principals from low-profile, flexible schools also describe how they make decisions in less stringent environments with fewer external pressures.

Change in a High-Profile, Traditional Environment

Many principals shared about being aware of potential limitations, in the form of opposition from stakeholders and influential decision makers both within the school and outside the school. In particular, principals in reputable, traditional high schools made decisions in very high-profile environments and recognized that at any time their decisions could be challenged by a central office administrator, a school committee member, or a reporter from the local newspaper. Decisions, therefore, had to be carefully crafted and well thought through so that the impact of the decisions on alumni, school committee, or school board members could be taken into consideration.

Dr. Manning (MA) described the culture at her elite, traditional high school. "We have educated signers of the declaration of independence. We don't jump on everything that comes down the pike." She added that her predecessor valued stewardship and maintaining tradition. Novel ideas were not readily adopted. However, Dr. Manning also emphasized the importance of preparing her students for a changing world. While Dr. Manning is cognizant of maintaining the traditions at her school, she has also elected to support proposals for new courses and embrace changes in pedagogy. Dr. Manning has carefully introduced these initiatives given her school's cautious approach to change. Even though a principal notices a host

> "We have educated signers of the declaration of independence. We don't jump on everything that comes down the pike." Principal Manning (MA)

of changes that should be implemented, unless faced with dramatically underperforming students, unscrupulous faculty behavior, or a crisis, multiple changes in such a tradition-laden environment should not be undertaken simultaneously. Introducing more than two changes in a year could be perceived as a precipitous approach to change.

Another aspect of Dr. Manning's school culture included her parents' predilection for communicating with central office leaders and local politicians to express their displeasure about school policies or procedures. When Dr. Manning made decisions and introduced change, she was aware that she was operating in a highly politicized environment where her school was closely scrutinized by parents, politicians, and the media.

Dr. Manning made the decision to shield her school from unwelcome publicity that could be misconstrued and potentially damaging to her students. Dr. Manning recounted a story about a young female student who impetuously tweeted about wanting to kill her teacher and who was subsequently assigned a fitting consequence. When the threat was assessed, it was determined that the student did not have the means nor had she developed a plan to carry out the threat. Dr. Manning was perturbed by the public nature of student mistakes and the potential impact on her school's reputation. When the incident occurred, she worried that the local newspaper would learn about the situation and that the student would be lambasted in the media, and as a result, the school's reputation would be tarnished. In this particular case, given the actions taken and the decisions made by Dr. Manning and her faculty, there was no publicity surrounding the incident.

Principal Henry (NC) described the culture of his diverse 100-year-old traditional high school and mentioned that his school is also competitive and extremely political. Since Mr. Henry acknowledges that many of the incidents that take place at his high-profile school will be featured in the media, he makes sure that he knows what is going on in his large high school so he is able to answer questions if asked and protect his students and staff. He talked about the challenges of entering a culture that is closed in some aspects to outsiders. In this type of environment, principals are faced with a school community where history is important, alumni wield political and economic power, and longstanding relationships are paramount. It could take an inordinate amount of time for a newcomer to be accepted, if at all. To operate successfully, principals need to understand why certain structures, policies, and systems are in place, and numerous inquiries should be made before changes are implemented. In Chapter 6, Principal Henry outlines his decision to fire a popular football coach and what he learned about his school's culture through subsequent reactions, including the impact of powerful alumni on his decision making. Mr. Henry indicated that he feels enormous pressure to maintain the level of academic success that his school has already achieved or to increase its performance. He cautiously approaches change, adding, "If you try to do something that is out of the box, you hear about it for two years straight." Based on the cultures of their elite traditional schools, both Dr. Manning and Principal Henry recognized the need to move slowly with major changes and decisions.

Change in a Low-Profile, Flexible Environment

Two other principals recalled what they had learned about the culture in their small, urban and suburban schools and how what they learned affected their decision making. Ms. Lily (MA) stated, "The culture is one in which the kids generally feel safe. There's a friendly rapport and banter with the teachers." While it was evident that safety and relationships with students were priorities in her small high school, she also added that "there is in some pockets a belief that we should get different students rather than wrap our arms around students and teach them." That is, some of the staff focus on changes that are outside their control—moving students rather than the changes within their control—transforming pedagogy, structures, and policies. Given what Ms. Lily observed about her school's culture and her own sense of changes that needed to be introduced, Ms. Lily relayed her decision to develop an academic support period for failing ninth- and tenth-grade students in her majority-minority urban school. In Chapter 4, Ms. Lily explains that every ninth- and tenth-grade teacher in her school is assigned to monitor a support class period. Through this model, students are able to receive additional instruction during the school day. This student intervention focuses on transforming pedagogy and school structures.

> "That is the kind of school where I'd like my child to go to: where the teachers know the kids." Principal Bliden (MA)

At his school, Mr. Bliden (MA) also stated that he and his faculty pride themselves on being very deliberate in focusing on relationships. Mr. Bliden is outside every day in front of the school greeting his students. Administrators put personalized notes on report cards for all 922 students. Teachers show up to games and performing arts events. Mr. Bliden mentioned that teachers are "able to pick up on when a kid is sliding and when a kid is not fully themselves. That is the kind of school where I'd like my child to go to: where the teachers know the kids." The culture at Mr. Bliden's school is congruent with his own belief in the importance of building personal relationships, connecting with students, and monitoring academic performance. When a new student from a school in Colorado arrived midyear as a result of a parent job transfer, Mr. Bliden made the decision to invest in developing a relationship with the new student. He e-mailed the student and asked him to stop by to see him. Mr. Bliden remarked that the student was surprised to hear from him and that he may not have known his former principal coming from a school of 3,200 students; but Mr. Bliden wanted to make sure the student knew him.

As principals make decisions, they take into consideration the culture of their respective buildings. Unlike the principals from highly traditional schools, neither Ms. Lily nor Mr. Bliden referenced making decisions in an environment with a strong alumni presence, parental resistance, or external pressure. In their schools, there appeared to be a degree of freedom to experiment in their decision making without encountering a high level of scrutiny. They also focused on how the size of their schools allowed them to be conscientious about improving relationships.

Laying the Groundwork for Effective Change

The next section of this chapter includes further decisions principals made to introduce change into the school culture by building trusting relationships and strategically introducing change.

Build Trusting Relationships

Principals were asked to describe the culture of their schools and to explain how the school's culture affected their decision making. It became evident from speaking to principals that for many of them, their established relationships with faculty and other stakeholders facilitated their ability to make difficult decisions about changing school culture. As a former principal, I also recognize the value of fostering strong working relationships with faculty and how those connections augmented my ability to spearhead change and execute decisions.

> "Ms. Prince told me that I was all about business. When I came into her classroom, I was always conducting a walkthrough or taking notes."

When I was a principal, in an effort to improve my relationships with teachers and also to gain some understanding about how I was perceived by staff, I invited Ms. Prince, a classroom teacher, to meet with me and tell me about her sense of my leadership style. Not many of us are fortunate enough to be told how we are actually viewed by our staff or colleagues. We may be told what we want to hear or have criticism couched in niceties. Ms. Prince told me that I was all about business. When I came into her classroom, I was always conducting a walkthrough or taking notes. From her vantage point, I rarely visited her classroom just talk to her about how she was doing. I realized after that frank conversation that I needed to spend more time getting to know my staff and building relationships. Thereafter, I shifted my attention from solely conducting evaluative classroom visits to investing time just getting to know the teachers in my building. Developing supportive, trusting relationships with teachers became a priority. Well known for his research on organizational culture and change, Fullan (2008) touts the importance of relationship-building in his framework of change. One of Fullan's six secrets of change is love your employees.

Loving your employees includes establishing authentic, caring relationships.

Major Areas That Affect School Climate

1. Safety

2. Relationships

3. Teaching and Learning

4. Institutional Environment

Source: National School Climate Council (2007).

In addition to relationships, other areas that affect school culture or climate include safety, teaching and learning, and the school environment.

Several principals described having a collaborative, close-knit culture in which they had developed strong relationships with faculty and staff. Ms. Cantrell (MA) added, "We have a very collaborative culture that promotes community. It goes along with my commitment to seek input from others and keep them informed. There are easy opportunities for me to get input from the faculty." In addition to relationships, other areas that affect school culture or climate include safety, teaching and learning, and the

> "My goal is for every teacher, custodian, and student to wake up and want to come to Sumpter High School." Principal Edwards (NC)

school environment. Ms. Cantrell has established a culture of inclusion by involving teachers in decisions and considering their perspectives when she makes decisions. Ms. Cantrell indicated that she remembers being a first-year teacher and all the mistakes that she made. She keeps that in mind when she is dealing with a teacher.

As a former coach, Mr. Edwards (NC) recognizes the importance of establishing close-knit, collaborative, trusting relationships at his school. Mr. Edwards added, "We have a very family-like atmosphere. My goal is for every teacher, custodian, and student to wake up and want to come to Sumpter High School (pseudonym) every morning, and they'll perform better." Mr. Edwards makes decisions that take into consideration his priority of relationship building and instituting a school climate that is characterized by a positive work environment.

When faced with making a decision about whether or not to permit his students to produce a lipdub (lipsync) video that would be filmed at school, Mr. Edwards consented. The lipdub video sponsored by his Student Government Association resulted in improved morale and brought together a cross-section of student participants.

As these principals spoke about how they had established trusting relationships with teachers in their buildings, they also attested to creating an environment of mutual respect whereby divergent perspectives were encouraged, open communication was invited, collaborative work was prioritized, and teachers and other staff members were treated like family. As we will see, it is vital to build such a climate of trust before attempting to introduce change.

Strategically Introduce Change

Change can be incredibly difficult. As Dr. Manning (MA) stated, "I always underestimate how hard change is for people and that my decisions often make an individual or a group change."

Before introducing changes, it is advisable to conduct a needs assessment of the school and not make changes until what is already working becomes apparent. Principals shared about clearly articulating the need for change, encouraging teachers to be part of the change, and developing a plan to move forward.

A strategy for changing the school culture is to set the right tone so that the culture will be reflective of the mission. If the school's mission involves high expectations, positive relationships with kids, and consequences for bad choices, it is important to model appropriate behavior and make decisions that are in line with those beliefs. If we

> "Listen to the children. They don't usually get to say what works best for them." Principal Wallace (MD)

raise our voice with students likely they will raise their voice with us. Principals who are mindful of their impact on school culture and change model desired behaviors, particularly behaviors that mirror the school mission. What is described here as modeling, Fullan (2011) would call deliberative doing. As he writes, the "effective change leader actively participates as a learner in helping the organization improve" (p. 5). The change or improvement is facilitated by intentional and reflection actions.

Principal Wallace (MD) stated that her priority is meeting the needs of her students. Ms. Wallace believes that if she meets student needs, everything else will work out. Ms. Wallace also indicated that she made decisions based on feedback from students. "For me, if you were hungry, I had to feed you. Listen to the children. They don't usually get to say what works best for them. I empower them to be advocates of their own education." Ms. Wallace believes that her students have a right to request a teacher conference if they believe that they are not being educated effectively. "Whether the teacher changes the style or not, they have to consider it. A lot of teachers don't like it. I am very service-oriented."

Principal Wallace has focused on how she can change the culture of her school by getting her entire staff to be more service-oriented. She has noticed that she sees more teachers meeting with parents and children processing issues together. Principal Wallace is confident that the meetings will help teachers be more sensitive to the needs of her students. "I don't want a parent to feel uncomfortable walking into a schoolhouse. There were days that principals gave me tough love as a parent and they said, trust me as the school leader." Principal Wallace formerly served on the local parent advisory committee for 4 years before becoming a principal. She explained that her work with parents and students is what drives a lot of her passion.

> "I always underestimate how hard change is for people and that my decisions often make an individual or a group change." Principal Manning (MA)

It is not always possible to implement change without making staffing changes. Ms. Perez (MA) changed the culture at her high school by hiring new teachers over a 4-year period who were supportive of the school's vision. She also changed structures within the school in order to create more opportunities for instructional collaboration during faculty meetings and during the school day. Ms. Perez made scheduling changes to allow teachers to have common planning time and she encouraged teachers to use data to develop common goals. Ms. Perez has also reduced the number of announcements made during faculty meetings and has begun to utilize more faculty meeting time for curriculum and instruction.

Changing Unsettling Environments

In addition to building trusting relationships with teachers and planning for the strategic introduction of change, principals recognized that sometimes dramatic and immediate changes are needed to regain control of a school. After highlighting aspects of their school's culture that were deplorable, principals shared strategies they utilized to implement change in their school's culture. Principal Rollins (MD) described the culture in his school before he introduced significant changes:

> One of the worst days was when students were throwing urine balloons at teachers. We had to shut down the school. I didn't have a mission and a vision. It took a year and a half to get it better. The first thing I did was bring the teachers together. I said I don't want to get hit with a urine balloon, and I don't think you do either. Here are some ideas I have, what do you think? It all started with a senior prank. I called an emergency faculty meeting. I shut down offices. I asked teachers to help patrol the halls. We wanted to know where every kid was at all times. Even though the students outnumber us, we were able to manage the school. We have not had that type of issue (again). It took bringing everybody together.

Mr. Rollins examined the culture at his urban school and the aspects of his school's culture that allowed repugnant incidents to be promulgated and an unsafe environment to be created. Immediate action was needed. After developing a plan for substantial improvements, Mr. Rollins encouraged faculty input, and then they determined together how to move forward and monitor their plan of improvement.

> "I called an emergency faculty meeting. I shut down offices. I asked teachers to help patrol the halls." Principal Rollins (MD)

Tips for Regaining Control of Unsettling Environments

1. Identify the culture at your school, the desired changes, and the potential impact on a proposed plan.

2. Develop a plan for substantial improvements.

3. Identify support and resources needed to implement the plan, including budgetary considerations, law enforcement, social service agencies, central office support, and so on.

4. Meet with faculty to provide input about the plan.

5. Monitor the implementation of the plan. Make adjustments as necessary.

At Principal Jeffreys's (MD) school, there were significant issues with gangs, violence, and intentionally set fires. Dr. Jeffreys stated, "We have seven gangs in one building. Trying to stop much of the nonsense. We didn't at the time have metal detectors. Every now and then we'd have a search. You'd already know who had something. It would be the kids who never came into school."

Dr. Jeffreys determined that it was important not only to have a balanced environment where students were comfortable and they could express themselves, but also to have rules in place to keep students safe. Dr. Jeffreys explained that it was important to make sure that her students understood the difference between what they could do in the street and what they could do in school. As a new principal, she said, she believed all the theory that suggested that if she established a quality environment, problems with behavior would dissipate. Changing the environment at her school was more complicated than following a simple formula.

> "You name it, we had it. There was a time we evacuated three to four times a day."
> Principal Jeffreys (MD)

Dr. Jeffreys described the environment at her school that had spiraled out of control. "There would be weapons, knives and things under tires in the parking lot. Just mob fights. You name it, we had it. There was a time we evacuated three to four times a day." Dr. Jeffreys discovered that students with a gang rivalry could attack one another during the time the school was being evacuated so students were pulling fire alarms to trigger an evacuation. At one point, students started setting real fires. Because of the frequency with which they were visiting her school, the fire department told Dr. Jeffreys that if she did not see an actual fire that the fire department was not going to require her school to evacuate.

Dr. Jeffreys instituted change by working collaboratively with her staff, the police department, and other outside agencies. Part of the plan they developed included guarding doors to prevent nonstudents from getting into the building. The staff also worked hard to become a school of choice by recruiting students who wanted to attend their school. Social workers and psychologists also were hired to support students, and the school coordinated a community rally.

Dr. Jeffreys was pleased that her students communicated that they too wanted to see a change in their school. Her school's reputation has improved such that her students now have a reputation for thinking that they are better than students at other city schools.

Summary

This chapter focused on the impact of school culture on decisions to introduce change. At a minimum, principals should take into consideration the culture of the school, then lay the groundwork for effective change: Relationships should be established and then change should be thoughtfully introduced. As Mr. Starnes (MA) asserted, "If you're making a decision without a really good understanding about the culture of the school and what decisions other leaders have made in that institution and how those decisions were viewed, you're operating in a deficit." A critical element of decision making is the capacity to be reflective and thoughtful. Reflection is especially vital if principals are implementing change.

4

Examining the Whole Picture

How is the decision going to impact our environment?
How is it going to impact people (adults on our campus)?
How is it going to impact students—the learning environment?

Mr. Peppers, Principal—North Carolina

In addition to assessing their core values and the culture of their school, principals examined the level of complexity or difficulty of their decisions and reviewed potential ramifications before deciding whom to involve and how to reach a collaborative solution. In taking this whole-picture perspective, principals also considered who would be affected by the decision (adults on campus as well as students), and some considered whether consensus building would be appropriate. The practices described above are analogous with Davis's (2004) practices that he asserts increase heuristic decision making.

Heuristic Decision Making

Davis (2004) juxtaposes rational decision making with heuristic decision making, writing that highly rational leaders are mythologized as leaders that deconstruct and carefully analyze problems and do not allow pressure or conflicts to negatively impact their sense of good judgment. Davis contends that in the everyday life of a school leader, such logical, structured decision making rarely occurs. Decisions that involve people can be complicated and unpredictable. Problems that are nebulous, controversial, unfamiliar, confusing, and multifaceted are least likely to be solved with analytical, rational thinking. In fact, given the nature of decision making in schools, such problems can be so volatile that poorly made decisions can make matters worse and trigger unintended negative consequences. Rational decision making in education is best suited for making decisions about quantitative data or budgets or completing routine tasks. Critical decisions can rarely be solved by following precise, preplanned steps.

As an alternative, Davis (2004) recommends using heuristic decision making. **Heuristic decision making** is defined as "preconceived responses to thematically similar problem situations" and Davis acknowledges that this makes heuristic decisions "susceptible to error" (p. 632). Heuristic thinking is further described as cutting "problems down to size by chunking patterns of information into easily managed pieces or rules of thumb. By rules of thumb it is meant that information is organized mentally via predetermined metarules that are category based and whole pattern in structure" (p. 631). Improving the ability to think heuristically is increased through reflection and making predictions about a likely course of events. Developing preconceived responses to similar problems should not be confused with developing preconceived responses to exact situations.

Some of Davis's (2004) practices for improving heuristic decision making, which fall under the umbrella of examining the whole picture, include Thinking Big, Expanding the Field of Attention, and Visualizing Solutions. In the interview comments below, there is a connection between the factors principals mention as they talk about difficult decisions and the practices that Davis specifies in his description of heuristic decision making.

> Heuristic decision making: Cutting "problems down to size by chunking patterns of information into easily managed pieces or rules of thumb."

Thinking Big

Thinking big describes the ability to view the entire scope of the situation and uncover large patterns. Principal Vance (NC) explained what he considers when making difficult decisions. "I look at the big picture. I find myself talking out loud literally, and I can hear in my head the response, and I try to carry myself through various scenarios so I am somewhat prepared." Mr. Bliden (MA) concurred, "I try to think about the problem at hand—the core problem. What are people really upset about? I do a dry run in my head, and I also do that out loud." When faced with difficult decisions, it is important for principals to explore all aspects of the problem and consider multiple scenarios while they are envisioning feasible alternatives. One strategy is talking out loud about plausible options with another administrator present. Several principals mentioned that they utilize this strategy. Principals also conveyed the importance of sifting through superfluous details to obtain a clear understanding of the core problem before making a decision.

> "I find myself talking out loud literally, and I can hear in my head the response." Principal Vance (NC)

Tips for Thinking Big

1. Explore all aspects of the problem. (Include multiple perspectives from all affected stakeholders.)
2. Consider alternative resolutions.
3. Bypass superfluous details. Identify the core problem(s).
4. Talk out loud with another administrator about the potential solution.

Expanding the Field of Attention

Another of Davis's (2004) recommendations is expanding the field of attention, which includes viewing the foreground and background of a dilemma and noticing the absence of critical information. Ms. Lily (MA) added, "I always want to make sure to see from various perspectives. What am I missing? When other people share—what is the angle when you hear contradictory stories? I visualize the obstacles and the negative consequences for the community." It is important to fully understand the dilemma so that as a decision is being made, all crucial factors are investigated and contradictions and competing interests are identified.

Principal Vance (NC) recounted, "I noticed I had an exorbitant amount of discipline issues that surrounded disrespect. When we surveyed the students, about 30% strongly agreed that adults treated them with respect. Only 25% of students said that students treat adults with respect." Principal Vance recalled viewing data from 697 respondents. There are 755 students and 47 teachers at his school.

> "I always want to make sure to see from various perspectives. What am I missing?"
> Principal Lily (MA)

Principal Vance could have scanned the discipline data and given a perfunctory response. Instead he chose to expand his field of attention by surveying students and implementing a strategy to address the underlying issues, one of which was students behaving disrespectfully to adults because they did not believe that adults respected them. One of the decisions Principal Vance made was to require students to watch a 20-minute video, the Butterfly Circus, and subsequently engage students in discussions about the meaning of respect. Principal Vance sought to discover information about perspectives that were missing from the data, namely student views. His efforts led to an improved climate in his school.

Tips for Expanding the Field of Attention

1. Identify the foreground of a dilemma (what you know).

2. Identify the background of the dilemma (what you would like to know—the details that are not obvious). This could include history, school culture, political impact, and potential for media involvement.

3. Identify obstacles.

4. Determine the perspectives of directly affected stakeholders.

5. Consider perspectives of indirectly affected stakeholders.

Visualizing Solutions

Davis (2004) also recommends envisioning a solution. This includes the development of a plan of action, rationale, alternate solutions, and consideration for how the resolution will be perceived. Ms. Perez (MA) stated, "I think when there's a dilemma, and you're thinking about a solution, you want to imagine the full outcome. Sometimes decisions don't take much time to make, but it takes more time to figure out what to do. More time for the planning." Ms. Perez contemplated how she solves pressing problems and formulates a solution. Ms. Perez emphasized the importance of

> "When there's a dilemma, and you're thinking about a solution, you want to imagine the full outcome." Principal Perez (MA)

planning while also acknowledging that at times it is difficult to predict all likely options.

Given the hectic pace of the principalship, it can be difficult to find time to visualize solutions. When I was a principal, I remember sleeping with a notepad beside my nightstand so if I woke up with a resolution, I could record the ideas even if I was not quite lucid when the idea was first formulated. If a decision is contem-

> "My best thinking comes when I'm driving home. I don't struggle with the decision once I've made it." Principal Jeffreys (MD)

plated for an extended period of time during the day, multiple solutions may come to the forefront in the wee hours of the night or morning. Sometimes principals ponder the solution to a challenging decision long after the school day has ended. The best time to dedicate to visualizing solutions depends on personal preference. One option is to come to work an hour before other staff members arrive with the express purpose of reflecting on the previous day's events. Principal Jeffreys (MD) presented an alternative, "My best thinking comes when I'm driving home. I don't struggle with the decision once I've made it. The best response is the best decision for everybody." In addition to planning, a critical element of formulating a solution includes developing a rationale. Principal Jeffreys mentioned that her rationale is based on decision making that benefits all her stakeholders, and she intimated that the quietness of the drive home leads to effective decision making. Principals can improve their ability to think heuristically and thereby make more effective decisions by examining the whole picture, which includes thinking big, expanding their field of attention, and visualizing solutions.

Tips for Visualizing Solutions

1. Develop a plan of action.

2. Articulate a rationale.

3. Consider how the resolution will be perceived.

4. Generate alternate solutions.

Is This a Complex Decision? A Difficult Decision?

In addition to exploring the whole picture, principals assessed the level of complexity or difficulty of the decision before deciding who else to involve. Some decisions are difficult, but not complex. Ms. Perez (MA) asserted, "I had to make a reduction in the number of teachers because of student enrollment. It was difficult to decide which teachers to cut, and it was difficult to listen to people talking about it (and not agreeing)." Ms. Perez indicated that reducing the number of teachers based on enrollment in different language courses was not a complex decision, but a difficult one, in that it caused disagreements among staff. Decisions can be difficult when there is a lack of resources or when the outcome will affect the lives of faculty or staff in a negative way.

Some more complex decisions might involve multiple factors—like figuring out an adequate schedule before submitting a budget—but might not be particularly difficult. Ms. Perez (MA) added, "I think that it is complex because you want to make sure you hire exactly what you need or otherwise you're wasting money. I want to maximize class size to an appropriate level. I don't want classes with 10 students in them."

> "What makes decisions difficult? The gray. Making sure I am fair and consistent and ethical. When it is not black and white. Sometimes in administration, there is a lot of gray." Principal Major (NC)

When asked what made a decision difficult, the interviewees mentioned a host of factors, including dissension among staff, lack of resources, tight timelines, the potentially negative affect of the decision on faculty and staff, and unclear ethical boundaries. Difficult decisions can have long-term implications such as scheduling, budget cuts, and teacher performance. Ms. Major (NC) mused, "What makes decisions difficult? The gray. Making sure I am fair and consistent and ethical. When it is not black and white. Sometimes in administration, there is a lot of gray."

What Makes Decisions Difficult?

Long-term implications, e.g., scheduling, budget cuts, teacher performance

Clear resolution is obscured

Lack of resources

Potential for negative impact on faculty or staff

Limited time to make the decision

Is This Decision a No Brainer?

Of course, not all decisions are either difficult or complex; some are simply "no brainers." Easy decisions include decisions to allow students to participate in experiences that would be beneficial academically or decisions clearly in the best interest of students. Other decisions are easy because of the requirements to follow policy or the necessity of assigning budgetary allotments based on prescribed criteria for personnel.

Dr. Manning (MA) explained that an easy decision is: "Will I let the kid who was invited to the National Biology Symposium go and present her paper? Sure." Mr. Starnes (MA) stated, "The easiest decisions are (easy because) it is so clearly in the best interest of kids that it is easy to make a decision in a certain way. It isn't always what the kids want." If a teacher wants to take a field trip during exam week, it would be an easy decision to deny the request.

Mr. King (NC) believes that decisions about budget allotments are easier because there is very little latitude regarding how to make the decision, particularly if the decision is made based on class size policy or state guidelines about allotments. Mr. King mentioned, "The easiest decisions are the ones with no gray areas—assigning teachers to positions. You have an allotment. You have so many teachers—assigning teachers to those areas."

> "The easiest decisions are (easy because) it is so clearly in the best interest of kids."
> Principal Starnes (MA)

Some easy decisions may not be easy to implement. Principals shared their experiences implementing new programs targeted toward improving student achievement. They believed that making the decision was easy, but implementation was challenging. Mr. Edwards (NC) shared, "My first year, we implemented a senior project. It was easy because I knew it was good for the kids. It was the easiest decision, but there were a lot of headaches. I knew what I wanted to do."

What Impact Will There Be on Faculty and Staff?

In addition to viewing pertinent aspects relative to the whole picture and determining the level of difficulty or complexity of a decision, principals also considered how faculty and staff would respond to decisions and how they would be affected by them. They paused to weigh the human impact as they moved toward a resolution and anticipated emotional responses.

As principals contemplate how decisions will impact faculty and staff, it is important to consider what faculty already know about a potential decision and what they should know given how they will be impacted by the decision. Ms. Cantrell (MA) added, "I don't like people to make decisions for me. My philosophy is to treat others as you want them to treat you. I try to inform others, give them advance notice, seek their opinion." Since Ms. Cantrell does not like others to make decisions for her, she tries not to make decisions for her staff. Whenever possible, she includes her staff in decisions that affect them.

Mr. Edwards (NC) explained that he has learned something from every supervisor. He also added that he applies a principle that he learned from his dad: "The golden rule, treat people how you want to be treated." When Mr. Edwards had to nonrenew a teacher who had worked at his school for a number of years, he communicated his decision in a way that was compassionate. "It was a budget reason. He (the teacher) didn't like what happened, but he respected how I handled it." Being compassionate is important to Mr. Edwards, so he makes sure that his decisions reflect his caring for staff even when difficult decisions have to be made.

> "I try to inform others, give them advance notice, seek their opinion." Principal Cantrell (MA)

Involving Others in the Decision-Making Process

After examining the big picture and determining the scope of the decision, principals made decisions about garnering input from faculty. In general, the interviewed principals were inclined to include faculty and staff in their decision making, and some incorporated faculty involvement more formally in the process.

Dr. Zenga has developed clearly established norms with her Leadership Team about how they involve others in decision making.

If Dr. Zenga is making a decision unrelated to her core values, she utilizes consensus building. For budget-related staffing decisions, Dr. Zenga engages her staff in a multiday process. Eighty percent of her staff are generally able to reach consensus. In the end, it is the last 20%, when they might have competing demands as they consider adding positions. When that happens, the ground rules established are that everyone can articulate a budgetary need, but they have to argue for someone else's department. They cannot argue for their own department. Dr. Zenga believes strongly that it is generally possible to get to 80% to 90% consensus on any given decision, and then someone needs to be the decisive leader. It can get very frustrating if decisions are not made. In the end, Dr. Zenga thanks staff for their participation then she becomes the decisive leader. She makes her decision and explains her thinking to her staff.

Mr. Starnes (MA) stated that when possible, he tries to build consensus, but he makes it clear that he is gathering data and that in the end he will make the final decision. Mr. Starnes described the process he engages in with reference to Dufour's (2007) definitions of loose and tight leadership. "This leadership approach fosters autonomy and creativity (loose) within a systematic framework that stipulates clear, nondiscretionary priorities and parameters (tight)." Dufour adds that the most critical element of loose and tight leadership is "getting tight about the right things" (p. 39). Mr. Starnes,

> "I try to create an environment that is loose. People have a lot of authority to make decisions." Principal Starnes (MA)

who subscribes to this philosophy, continued, "I try to create an environment that is loose. People have a lot of authority to make decisions in areas in which they have authority and use me as a sounding board, but not to come and get answers from me." Mr. Starnes worries that the downfall is that sometimes he may not push his staff as hard or as fast as he could because he does not micromanage them. Mr. Starnes added that he prefers to work in an environment where his staff are making better decisions, not necessarily less risky decisions.

Principal Rollins (MD) also encourages his staff members to be part of the decision-making process, stating that his approach is very collaborative and that he does not make decisions without involving people who are affected. When problems arise, Mr. Rollins stated, "I bring in the people who are directly impacted.

> "I bring in the people who are directly impacted. I bring my assistant principals and teachers in, and now I'm starting to bring students in." Principal Rollins (MD)

I bring my assistant principals and teachers in, and now I'm starting to bring students in."

The decision-making processes that these principals implement are in accordance with what Spillane and Healey (2010) have described as a distributed leadership perspective that includes two facets, the "leader plus" and "practice." The leader plus aspect acknowledges that others in addition to the principal can be included in the leadership and management of schools. Leader plus also focuses on identifying who is included and how collaborative leadership is conducted. Leadership practice highlights the practice of leading and managing, and the interaction between team members who bring different expertise. Principals interviewed indicated that they utilize distributive leadership. In particular, principals recognized the importance of including many voices of staff and other stakeholders in their decision making when possible. Principals clearly valued the importance of faculty and staff input; however, they also expressed the need to be strategic about when to involve others.

On a related issue—consensus building—the principals reported reservations about how much time to spend unpacking a decision through consensus and about which decisions should be resolved using consensus. There are limitations with consensus building. With consensus, faculty and staff are going to be heard, but the results may be different than they desire or anticipate. Involving faculty and staff in decision making is not equated here with consensus building, but it is mentioned as a subset of distributed leadership practices.

Involving Teachers and Parents: A Special Education Change

Mr. Starnes (MA) shared his experience working with faculty to restructure the **exceptional education** department at his affluent suburban school.

> "It was challenging because you're dealing with our most fragile students and parents who are very knowledgeable about the process." Principal Starnes (MA)

In an effort to intentionally involve **Special Education** teachers and parents in the decision-making process, Mr. Starnes coordinated meetings with teachers and conducted a parent input session. "I completely restructured the Special Education department because we were reducing our budget. It came out of a belief that we weren't serving kids. It was challenging because you're dealing with our most fragile students and parents who are very knowledgeable about the process."

In addition to meeting with teachers and parents, Principal Starnes contracted an outside consultant to provide input on restructuring. Through that data gathering, Principal Starnes reduced his school's exceptional education staff by seven people, which was a 10% reduction. He measured the success of the restructuring by noting that parents seemed to be pleased with the changes. The following year, no parents of Special Education children complained that their child's needs were not being met as a result of the reduction. Co-teaching was also added. The exceptional education staff supported the assertion that there was a better way to serve Special Education students in their school. The redesign process was challenging due to the high-stakes nature of decision making about Special Education, compliance with federal and state laws, and the complexity of the decisions that had to be made.

With these factors in mind, Principal Starnes recognized the importance of (1) including parents, teachers, and a knowledgeable consultant in the process and (2) proceeding cautiously with the adoption of the plan until he had garnered significant school and community support. It takes courage to implement a change of this magnitude in a wealthy town with a highly involved parent community. Parents and teachers needed reassurance that although there would be a substantial reduction in staff, service to students and compliance with individualized education program (IEP) goals would remain priorities.

Involving Counselors and Teachers: A Plan to Raise Student Achievement

When I was a high school administrator, I worked with a team of counselors, assistant principals, and teachers to develop and implement a plan to improve student achievement. I noticed that we had a large number of students—130+ school-wide—with two or more Fs. The CARE Team/Academic Plan process was implemented to reduce the number of student failures and to support higher academic achievement. For incoming ninth graders, systems were in place districtwide for counselors to confer regarding incoming students. I began meeting with high school counselors to review the list of incoming students and to develop an initial High School CARE Team list. Students were placed on the list based on attendance, behavior, or academics. Once the list was generated, each assistant principal and counselor met with students on their CARE Team list on a weekly basis. It became apparent fairly early on in the process that the students on the list were those students with whom an assistant principal would already be meeting on a regular basis due to disciplinary referrals or through crisis intervention. In many cases, the regularly scheduled weekly meetings between counselors or assistant principals and the student served to preempt the need for regular disciplinary referrals. Part of what contributed to the program's success was a tenacious commitment to individual weekly meetings with underperforming students, weekly meetings with the CARE Team counselor/administrator team, and an ongoing collaboration between faculty, counselors, and administrators. A preexisting structure also facilitated the program's success: a 50-minute common lunch, highly unusual for a 1,400-student school. Teachers were willing to give up most of that 50-minute lunch period on a daily basis to meet with students individually and in small groups. Weekly communication with the assistant principal and classroom teacher was an integral component of the program as was quarterly communication with all faculty and revisions to the list based on improved student performance. As a result of a number of collaborative meetings with faculty, counselors, and administrators, the CARE Team/Academic Plan Process listed in Table 4.1 was implemented.

Table 4.1   CARE Team/Academic Plan Process

Meet with middle schools to develop initial High School CARE Team list. Students are placed on list based on attendance, behavior, or academics.
In June, review list of students with two or more Fs as a final second semester grade. Add students to CARE Team list.
Develop a new CARE Team list of students based on academics, attendance, and/or behavior. Share CARE Team list with faculty for input and provide updates each quarter.
All students from the CARE Team list ~ 130 students are assigned to meet with a counselor or assistant principal (AP) on a weekly basis. At initial meeting, counselor or AP meets with CARE Team students to develop an Academic Plan.
Counselor or AP meets with CARE Team students to check on academic progress for that week and to confirm that the students met with teachers the previous week.
Students on the CARE Team list are required to meet with one or more teachers for tutoring/homework help during lunch or after school.
CARE Teams (counselor and APs) meet on a weekly basis about a specified group of students from the CARE Team list. Discuss support for students, weekly monitoring of academic plans, and required weekly meetings with teachers for remediation, especially Algebra I (Common Core Math I) and English I teachers.

PLATO (online course recovery) reteaching/remediation is mandatory.
List of interventions for students who fail is developed, e.g., guided study hall, Math Lab, or PLATO (for reteaching).
Students move out of an intervention, such as study hall, Math Lab, or PLATO, when it becomes evident that support is no longer needed (students demonstrate mastery of essential learning on a consistent basis).
At each quarter, continue to monitor students placed on CARE Team list and add/remove students to/from list as needed.
For students who have struggled in math, place them in Math Lab instead of study hall.
D and F list at progress report (Revise list and develop Academic Plans.)
Athletic coaches monitor athletes' academics weekly or biweekly, provide study halls for athletes, and bench athletes when grades are not satisfactory (passing grades).
Monthly meetings with coaches to monitor student athletes' grades.

Source: Developed by this author on February 9, 2010. Submitted as part of the Durham Public Schools, Durham Association of Educators, National Education Association (NEA) Foundation Closing the Achievement Gap Grant.

Consulting Mentors: Principals' Networks of Support

In addition to involving teachers and parents in decision making, principals shared their experience with another type of collaborative involvement—mentors who helped them successfully navigate the culture in their schools. Ms. Lyons (NC) asserted, "My mentor principal exposed me to every aspect that was possible in leadership and I think that is key—that we bring assistant principals in so if they have to go through that, they have base knowledge to make the correct decisions." Principal Rollins (MD) revealed, "I have help in most situations. I have a network of support that I have made over the years that I can call someone up and say, hey, this happened, what do you think?" Mr. Rollins further stated that he decides which mentor to talk to depending on the situation since the mentors all have different skill sets. "I remember I talked to one of my colleagues. I was struggling with culture and climate. This principal was a guru on culture and climate. He said he used lunch time to talk to his students." Mr. Rollins indicated that the mentor he talked to had a small school of 400 students. With 400 students in each of his lunches and four lunches, Mr. Rollins has the largest school in his district. The mentor gave him some good information, but the mentor could not help him with the execution because of size differences between their schools. Principals reflected on value of the support that they received and how they sifted through advice to make a good decision.

It is very helpful to establish rapport with experienced, trustworthy principals who have been successful in their positions. Experienced principals can advise new principals and help them avert making potentially disastrous decisions. Some decisions are not instinctive. New principals may not be able to predict that certain decisions will upset faculty or parents. When determining the best course of action, it is instructive to evaluate whether the decision is an easy decision or a difficult decision. An easy decision can be made relatively quickly with little consultation with others, but for a difficult decision the input of more experienced colleagues is invaluable.

Summary

When making decisions, principals generated viable solutions that encompassed expected outcomes, pitfalls, benefits, unintended consequences, and multiple scenarios (Davis, 2004). Principals also sought input from others when making decisions and assessed how their staff would be impacted by their decisions. Principals noted that staff feedback significantly influenced their decision making and that they paid particular attention to that feedback in cases when their decisions would directly impact their staff. The individuals whom principals selected to include in their decision making sometimes depended on the situation itself. In some cases, principals consulted mentors. Mr. Adams (NC), whose comments were reflective of most interviewees, stated that decisions can become difficult when they affect the lives of others so he tries very hard not to make decisions alone.

PART II

Making
Difficult Decisions

5

Decisions About Student Consequences

Students can make really bad decisions,
but it doesn't make them bad people.
Too often students are put into boxes and written off.
Students need consequences for their actions,
but we always push them to be their best selves.

Ms. Lily, Principal—Massachusetts

In Part I of this book, Chapters 1–4, I investigated the factors expert principals explore in decision making, namely, key problem-solving processes, core values, school culture, examining the whole picture, and involving faculty and mentors in decision making. In these remaining chapters, 5–8, I take a more in-depth look at specific types of decisions and present cases about particular difficult decisions these principals encountered and how they resolved them. Included are decisions about student consequences; budgeting and staffing;

programs, practices, and policies; and decisions that improve the performance of African American and Latino students.

Some of the most difficult decisions principals have to make are the result of poor student choices that require disciplinary action. In their interviews, principals shared that they were able to separate the behavior from the student and issue a consequence after careful investigation that considered school policy and the impact of the decision on students. Parents and students may not have always agreed with the consequences, but principals worked to ensure that parents and students at least understood their rationale.

In the two case studies at the close of this chapter, as well as in the experiences related by principals below, readers will have an opportunity to think through and discuss how they might handle potentially volatile situations that involve decisions about the assigning of consequences as well as related issues, including publicity, communication with parents and staff, and support for affected students.

Decisions About Student Consequences: Factors to Consider

Utilize key problem-solving processes

Reflect on core values

Consider school culture

Determine the human impact

Analyze the whole picture

Consult others

Managing a Crisis

In each of the three crises that are discussed in this section, including my own example, the principals articulated several actions that were necessary components of the decision-making process they had to undertake. Each principal conducted a thorough investigation and considered the impact of the law and school policy on their decisions. In addition, we all considered key problem-solving processes, our core values, school culture, the human impact; examined the whole picture; and consulted others before making a decision about the consequences of student behaviors.

Senior Prank—Sexually Explicit Notes

While I was working as an administrator at Northants Midlands High School, Keenan, a senior boy, left the following sticky notes on a teacher's desk: "Mr. Simpson likes transsexuals" and "Simpson loves men." Earlier in the school year, Keenan had created an empty "porn" icon on Mr. Simpson's desktop computer. Mr. Simpson had not reported the earlier incident to school administration. On the disciplinary form regarding the sticky notes, Mr. Simpson marked the following reasons for the referral: insubordination and harassment/ bullying. When I met with Keenan, he admitted the actions but claimed that both incidents were a joke. After meeting with Mr. Simpson and Keenan, I called Keenan's mother, Mrs. Winters, and notified her that Keenan would be suspended.

Mrs. Winters requested a meeting with me and Mr. Simpson to discuss Keenan's consequences. At the meeting, Mrs. Winters shared that her other son, also a student at Northants Midlands High School, had been harassed several times, but he did not report it. Essentially Mrs. Winters was questioning why Mr. Simpson had reported the incident. Mrs. Winters intimated that although this matter should be taken seriously, Keenan is a good kid and she could not understand why it was not apparent that Keenan was joking. He clearly crossed a line, but he had received mixed messages from Mr. Simpson. Referring to the previous incident about the porn folder, Mrs. Winters stated that nobody let her or her husband know what was going on. Mrs. Winters asked that this situation be treated as a warning and that the school find a way to help Keenan given that his actions were not malicious. After being told about the suspension, Mrs. Winters asked if Keenan could be given an in-school suspension instead.

Before issuing a consequence, I reviewed school policy and, based on the student handbook, Keenan's actions were deserving of a suspension. While it was true neither Mrs. Winters nor the administration had been made aware of the previous incident, it did not negate this current offense. As standard practice, our school did not issue warnings for this type of egregious behavior. I concurred that both Mrs. Winters and the administration should have been notified about the first incident and acknowledged that notification might have prevented a second incident from occurring. I also added that the prior incident would likely have resulted in a suspension as well. I informed Mrs. Winters about how a suspension could impact Keenan's college application process and made her aware that most colleges require prospective students to provide a written explanation about a suspension. Since the incident had taken place during soccer season and Keenan was a soccer player,

Keenan could also face possible game suspension from his coaches. It was a difficult meeting because serious consequences had to be issued based on a student's poor choices. I made it clear to the parent and the student that Keenan would be treated fairly. As a compromise, after talking to the teacher and receiving his support, the consequence was reduced to a 5-day in-school suspension instead of an out-of-school suspension.

In this instance, it was crucial to spend time gathering all the facts that pertained to Keenan's actions, his assessment of his actions, and Mr. Simpson's response. Parents are not typically consulted before issuing a disciplinary consequence, but in this situation, the parent's feedback about an unreported previous offense warranted consideration. In addition to reviewing a written disciplinary referral, I often consulted teachers before issuing a suspension if the student had made inflammatory remarks directed toward a teacher and multiple consequences were an option. Finally, fair and consistent consequences were issued that aligned with the student handbook. As is the case when making decisions about student disciplinary matters and illustrated above, it is essential to obtain all the facts through data gathering, consult school policy (handbook), and consider multiple perspectives.

A Racially Charged Fight Between Students

Ms. Langely (MA) described a fight between two male students, an African American male who was part of a regional voluntary desegregation program called **METCO** and a resident White male student. The fight carried over from an argument at a lunch table and spilled over outside in front of Ms. Langely's 1,900-student school.

> The most challenging part of the incident was communicating with the parents. The resident parents initially challenged Ms. Langely's decision to suspend their son, and the father made a veiled threat that he would follow legal action should the METCO student return to school.

Tempers flared. A potentially volatile situation erupted with hundreds of onlookers present, and videos were circulated throughout the school about the fight. Boston minority students and resident White students in this community have a history of very tense school-wide conflicts that are racially motivated and divisive. This community has also demonstrated a willingness to engage students in transparent discussions about race—a high school Social Studies course on antiracism has been taught as an elective to juniors and seniors for more than a decade. A thorough investigation revealed that prior to the fight there were several derogatory remarks directed at the METCO student about his GPA. The METCO student was the aggressor, but the resident student went beyond self-defense by punching the METCO student. After reviewing the evidence, which included interviewing students and teachers, examining the videos, and consulting the student handbook, Ms. Langely decided to suspend both boys. Ms. Langely spent hours sifting through evidence that included at least seven different versions of what took place at the lunch table. She was also quite aware of the racial dynamics involved in this incident. Ms. Langely suspended the METCO student for 10 days and suspended the resident student for 5 days. The most challenging part of the incident was communicating with the parents. The resident parents initially challenged Ms. Langely's decision to suspend their son, and the father made a veiled threat that he would follow legal action should the METCO student return to school. The resident parent wanted the METCO student to essentially be expelled. Ms. Langely recounted, "I received a call last week from the father who was demanding to know when the student was returning, and he said if that student returns, there will be a police officer at the METCO bus when that student returns, then he called the METCO director."

Since the METCO student was a Special Education student, Ms. Langely also conducted a **manifestation determination** and a reentry hearing. When the disciplinary consequence for a Special Education student includes the possibility of an alternative placement, suspension, or expulsion, a manifestation determination is conducted to determine the appropriate consequence and to assess whether the student's disability is a mitigating factor. Ms. Langely was concerned about the METCO student's decision to follow the resident student when he could have chosen to walk away. What complicated matters was that the evidence suggested that testing would be beneficial, but the METCO parents did not want to pursue Special Education testing because of fear of legal action. Depending on the type of tests and the results, the tests may have suggested the need for additional on-site supports or a change in school placement. The supports that the IEP team determined were needed were therefore not addressed. Ms. Langely indicated that the boys had moved on and were no longer having issues with one another. She mentioned that there are still some residual effects, but that it was a good learning experience for her, particularly regarding the Special Education process. She was also able to successfully navigate discussions about race that surfaced.

> **In the case of a racially charged fight that has the potential to cause a significant disruption to the school community, the following tips should be followed:**
>
> - Separate the students immediately and gather witness statements.
> - Review witness statements, consult the student handbook, and consider potential student, parental, and faculty responses to the consequences before issuing.
> - Consider the fairness of the consequences and anticipate that either or both parents could view the consequences as racially biased or simply unfair.
> - Consult the school attorney and Human Resources about potential ramifications that could have been overlooked.
> - Decide in advance. If there is a willingness to reduce the consequences for either or both parties, under what circumstances might the consequences be changed and how would the change be viewed by the other party once the change becomes public?
> - Prepare for reentry hearings. Provide mediation. Assign counselors and other administrators to monitor the two students to prevent any future reoccurrences.

Suspected Weapon on Campus

Dr. Zenga (MA) elucidated her experience with a crisis. A student in her school reported that another student was carrying a gun. Within 6 to 7 minutes of looking, it was clear that they could not locate the second student who ran off when a teacher asked what was going on. Dr. Zenga indicated that there was enough concern that there was a student in possession of a weapon so she made the decision to lock down the school immediately.

Though she consulted the police, it was made clear to her that the police were not going to make the decision about a lockdown. "I felt very strongly that I could only make one wrong decision, that would have been to have put my students into any jeopardy of their safety. I understood the ramifications of the media, the parents, the instructional ramifications (losing instructional time)."

The school was in lockdown as the police and the administration searched the community and the school for the student. After it was determined that the student was not in the building, Dr. Zenga moved to a shelter in place that allowed for some limited movement of classes within the building. Meanwhile Dr. Zenga had begun to send initial emergency calls to parents, and several news organizations were outside the school. That afternoon, the suspected student was found by police in town. He claimed that the student who reported seeing him with a gun had actually only seen a lighter. Local police reported that the student was in possession of a butane lighter that looked like a weapon.

There was a lot of anxiety intertwined in the decision to move to a lockdown. Dr. Zenga had to manage the short- and long-term decisions and manage the lockdown with the police, fire department, students, media, central office, and parents. Her students were also texting their parents. She had to manage the subsequent long voicemail to parents and the longer message to the media. The decision to move to a lockdown was the easier of those decisions. Dr. Zenga decided that the safety of her students was far more important that any ramifications from negative publicity.

There were a number of decisions that Dr. Zenga had to communicate to faculty, custodial staff, and the police. Dr. Zenga had already been principal for 5 years at this school when the crisis developed. She had prior experience closing the school for a bomb scare, and in her second year, a student had threatened her life. The press described the handling of the incident in a positive light and portrayed Dr. Zenga as a strong leader who was willing to make difficult decisions. Fortunately this crisis was managed well and the story played

> "I felt very strongly that I could only make one wrong decision, that would have been to have put my students into any jeopardy of their safety. I understood the ramifications of the media, the parents, the instructional ramifications (losing instructional time)." Principal Zenga (MA)

well in the media. Dr. Zenga was responsive, investigated the matter thoroughly, and made a timely decision based on the crisis. She also managed effective communication with law enforcement, central office, parents, students, staff, and the media. Dr. Zenga considered the big picture impact of how a lockdown would be viewed by parents, central office, and the outside community. The school district's Rights and Responsibilities handbook was utilized to determine how to handle consequences for the student who had left campus without permission and was at the center of the decision to place the school on lockdown.

Making Policy Changes

Sometimes principals felt compelled to make policy changes as a result of student choices. Principals shared the guidelines that they

> **Tips to Consider When Managing a Crisis With a Suspected Weapon or Actual Weapon on School Grounds**
>
> • Investigate quickly. Utilize administrators to gather pertinent data needed (including witness statements) to make the best decisions.
> • Consult the School Resource Officer and local law enforcement as necessary. Provide Central Office with an update.
> • Make decisions in the best interest of the entire school community, not just for one or two students. E-mail faculty about the incident.
> • Develop a plan to ensure that all students will be safe. Move students to classes or designated safety zones (away from the potential crisis) as quickly as possible.
> • Once the crisis has subsided, if the Incident impacts the entire school (lockdown), communicate a brief message to students via the public address system that assures them of their safety and provides some limited details about the incident.
> • Consult Central Office about communicating with the media and the language for the voicemail message that is sent to parents.
> • Send a voicemail to parents updating them on the crisis.
> • Announce more details to students via the public address system and send a more detailed e-mail message to faculty apprising them of developments.

consider in these situations. As was mentioned in Chapter 2, principals recognized the importance of being knowledgeable about school board/school committee policy, and they also considered existing policies as they introduced new policies based on student choices.

Temporarily Suspending School Dances

At Ms. Langely's large, affluent suburban high school in Massachusetts, school dances were a popular way for students to spend a weekend night. However, Ms. Langely recently made the difficult decision to temporarily suspend all school dances, after two students were taken by ambulance to the hospital with blood alcohol levels in the critical range. To compound the matter, it had become increasingly difficult to find faculty chaperones for the dances. Many students were overly sexual at the dances and openly disregarded faculty requests that they curtail their behavior. Dance

Tips to Consider When Making Policy Changes

- Become familiar with school/district policies that pertain to the changes that will be introduced.
- If policies will be revised, ensure that newly introduced policies do not violate laws or district polices.
- Articulate the rationale for the change including the improvements that will take place.
- Contemplate how the policy change operates in conjunction with or in opposition to your core values and/or the school's core values/mission.
- Investigate whether the proposed plan is currently being implemented in other schools inside or outside the district.
- Timing is everything. Consider whether this is the best time to implement a change.
- If applicable, meet with other principals about the implementation of their plan.
- Revisit Chapter 3: Considering the Culture Before Introducing Change.
- Meet with the faculty and administrative team for input on a proposed plan.
- Utilize the School Improvement Team to garner input from parents and students as applicable.
- Determine how the new policy will affect segments of the student population and the entire school body.

attendance had dropped from 250 to the same 100 students each time.

Ms. Langely ultimately decided to put school dances on hold for the first half of the year. She made her decision after consulting her faculty and her administrative team. Ms. Langely considered a host of factors, but her decision was based primarily on safety concerns. It was also informed by policy.

At Ms. Langely's school, the School Dance and Event Policy stipulates strict adherence to a substance abuse policy that prohibits the use of alcohol on campus. It also indicates that school dances are a privilege and students are expected to maintain respectful and appropriate behavior during the dances. Being intoxicated or refusing to comply with adult requests to cease overly sexual behavior violates this policy. Since the violations caused the dances to be temporarily suspended, a Breathalyzer Testing Procedures and Protocol was developed and added to the student/parent handbook. A faculty-student committee was charged with developing a plan to resolve the issues and make dances safer without putting in place a host of new rules. "We got caught in the flack with the Halloween GSA Dance, which has gone on without a hitch. There were a lot of meetings, but we were not going to say yes to this dance, but no to this dance." One of the challenges that Ms. Langely faced was that the school's popular Gay-Straight Alliance (GSA) Dance, which usually had no issues, was also canceled. The administration agreed that they would not choose to let some dances take place and cancel others.

> "There were a lot of meetings, but we were not going to say yes to this dance, but no to this dance." Principal Langely (MA)

All dances were canceled for the fall semester until the committee reached an acceptable resolution. It was a fairly drastic decision to temporarily suspend school dances, but as illustrated above, safety concerns were mounting and inappropriate behavior was ongoing. Since that temporary suspension of dances and the policy changes, dances have been scheduled again, behavioral expectations have been clarified, and chaperones are again volunteering.

Implementing Attendance Changes

Other policy changes described here include attendance changes. Principal Wallace (MD) discussed the attendance and tardy policy changes that she implemented to improve her students' work ethic and their level of responsibility. "Attendance is a huge issue. If you are going to be late, here is my cell phone and the front office phone number. I wanted to get them to a level of responsibility." Foremost among all the policy changes was the decision not to accept parent calls: She thanked parents when they called in an absence or tardy, but she followed up by reiterating her expectations that their son or daughter make the phone call. Her rationale? "When he gets a job, you won't be able to call for him. Ninety percent of my parents are on board. It is working. The students are really responsible. If they don't call in, I don't let them in." Students who arrive late to Ms. Wallace's alternative school are not allowed in if they have not called in advance. It takes a clear understanding of school culture, central office support, and relationship development before implementing changes of the magnitude that Principal Wallace reported. At first glance, these may appear to be minor changes. However, the decision not to accept parent phone calls or not to allow late students to enter the school is fairly radical and could have been met with fierce opposition.

Ms. Wallace also enhanced her school's job placement program by deciding to improve partnerships with local businesses and area hospitals. When Ms. Wallace first arrived at her school, no students had been

> "When he gets a job, you won't be able to call for him. . . . The students are really responsible. If they don't call in, I don't let them in." Principal Wallace (MD)

placed in jobs in 2 years. She shared her expectations with her staff, "I told him (teacher in charge of job placement), we needed 25 by the end of the year. I hired four students myself, and they help in the main office. That was a culture change. They had to do résumés. Be hired. You represent me. Now everyone is asking for a job and finding partnerships." As a result of meetings with administrators in local hospitals, hospitals now hire Ms. Wallace's students as medical assistants. Ms. Wallace has also developed a partnership with the local community college to establish a dual enrollment program that allows students to complete college credit while they are still in high school. Ms. Wallace is instilling responsibility in her students by creating expectations for attendance and tardiness that match those of an employer.

Recommending Long-Term Suspensions or Expulsions: Compassionate Enforcement

The decisions about student consequences described thus far have involved either managing a crisis (a racially charged fight and a suspected weapon on campus) or making decisions about policy changes (temporarily suspending school dances and implementing attendance changes). When faced with decisions that may or may not include crises or policy changes, but could result in long-term suspensions or expulsions, principals described themselves as compassionate enforcers of school policy. That is, they not only are guided by school board or school committee policy when determining consequences, but also consider the impact of their decisions on individual students as well as on the larger school community. Mr. Henry (NC) indicated that he considers the human impact of his decisions when he assigns consequences to students. He balances that consideration with being very clear and strict about enforcing policy, especially when the situation involves drug or alcohol violations. In Mr. Henry's county, a first-time alcohol/substance abuse violation could result in an in-school suspension or short-term suspension. Additional drug- or alcohol-related

Tips for Recommending a Long-Term Suspension or Expulsion

- Separate the behavior from the student and approach consequences objectively by adhering to school/district policy and state/federal laws.
- Investigate carefully using data-focused key problem-solving processes.
- Be compassionate while enforcing school board/school committee policies.
- Consider the impact of decisions on individual students and the school community.
- Determine whether a precedent is being set by the assigned consequences or if the consequence falls in line with policy.
- Follow meticulously the detailed district guidelines for recommending a long-term suspension/expulsion.

offenses (not including intent to distribute, which carries a more severe consequence) may result in disciplinary reassignment to an alternative program or long-term suspension.

Dr. Manning (MA) recounted her experience with a serious drug-related offense. "Expulsions are difficult because the decision is not in the best interest of the individual student, but I have to do what is the best interest of the rest of them. If I didn't, I wouldn't expel anyone." In Dr. Manning's district, expulsions are more common than long-term suspensions. Initial expulsions do not result in removal from the district, rather removal to another district school. According to Massachusetts General Law, Chapter 71, Section 37H, use or possession of drugs or alcohol may result in an expulsion. The Education Reform Act of 1993 describes circumstances that permit the principal (not the superintendent) to expel a student. One of those areas described in Massachusetts General Law, Chapter 71, Section 37H includes the possession of a controlled substance on school grounds.

Because suspensions and expulsions are serious consequences that affect students' futures, principals are particularly cognizant of the message that their assigned consequences send to faculty and the student body. Precedent setting was a factor. Similar considerations are expressed by principals in Chapter 6 related to making decisions about firing a popular coach. Consistency was also described as important especially since faculty members and other students are taking note of how suspensions and expulsions are handled. When making decisions that will result in suspensions or expulsions, principals should evaluate the impact of the behavioral violations and subsequent consequences on the entire school community.

Dr. Manning explained that she has come to realize in the past couple of years that even though she assigns students the same consequence for the same offense, her students can be profoundly affected in different ways. Dr. Manning mentioned that she had three students that were all caught in possession of marijuana. It is unclear if the students had a large enough quantity to be charged with intent to distribute. Dr. Manning's decision to expel the three students was an equal consequence, but the impact for each boy was very different. One boy had parents with lots of resources whose parents Dr. Manning surmised had enrolled their son in a fine private school. The penalty was more severe for another student, who would be a first-generation college student with limited financial resources. Because she was aware of the differing impact of her decision,

> "Expulsions are difficult because the decision is not in the best interest of the individual student, but I have to do what is the best interest of the rest of them. If I didn't, I wouldn't expel anyone." Principal Manning (MA)

Dr. Manning spent a considerable amount of time communicating with other district schools to help that student find another school (in the district). Being aware of how her decision impacted students differently did not mean assigning a lesser consequence. Instead it meant that this principal chose to provide her student with assistance navigating the school system to ensure that the student was appropriately placed in a challenging learning environment.

Principals considered the human impact when making decisions about student expulsions or long-term suspensions. Mr. King (NC) concurred. He considers the human impact of his decisions on the entire student body. "The first thing I consider is the kids, not one or two, the greater population because it sets a precedent because you have teachers who are observing it as it goes on." Mr. King also considers how his decisions about students are viewed by the faculty. Given the confidential and legal nature of most decisions involving students, he does not solicit teacher input. In

> "I never make a decision about discipline instantly because I like to have students reflect on their decisions." Principal Lyons (MA)

addition to considering the human impact, Mr. King conducts a thorough investigation and consults school board policy. "Teachers don't suspend so it is like being a detective and you start doing thorough investigating. If it's a suspension, easy policy manuals on that." The assigned consequences are determined by school policy.

Ms. Lyons (NC) shared her experience with a discipline incident involving drugs and a weapon. A student whom she described as bright and capable lost a year of his education at her school after being suspended for 365 days. Ms. Lyons continued, "I never make a decision about discipline instantly because I like to have students reflect on their decisions. Unless it is an emergency, a 911, then it's an instant decision. I try to do my research before I make my decision." It is important to provide students with an opportunity for reflection when poor choices are made in hopes that they will choose not to make a similar mistake in the future.

Summary

This chapter examined decisions that were made by principals in response to student behavior or choices that necessitated disciplinary consequences. Principals described how they managed crises, the challenge of recommending long-term suspensions or expulsions, and their adherence to school board policy and law. Sometimes decisions were straightforward and could be resolved by simply consulting the student handbook. In other cases, there were nuances to be considered. In all cases, principals contemplated the human impact of their decisions. Mr. Peppers (NC) mentioned that after years of experience as an administrator, he knows the importance of closely following school board policy. He relies on common sense and gets advice from others in his building and also from central services. Most significant, principals described themselves as compassionate enforcers of school policy. Ms. Cantrell (MA) said, "I still keep in my mind how it felt to be a student so when I am making decisions about how students learn or when I am dealing with a student on a discipline issue, I still remember what it was like."

Chapter 5 Case Studies

As you read the following cases, keep in mind the following general questions, in preparation for responding to more specific reflective questions at the close of each case:

- Develop a summary of what you know about what happened.
- Make a list of what else you would like to know.
- Imagine you were the principal of this high school, and think about how you would handle the situation and the many decisions to be made.

CASE STUDY #3

The Distorted Yearbook Picture

Helen, a tenth grader, moved to Morant Surrey High School and joined the field hockey team. Soon after her arrival at Morant Surrey High School, Helen and Mandy developed a contentious relationship that continued into their senior year. Mandy's dislike for Helen was partially based on Mandy's belief that Helen had been flirtatious with her boyfriend. Both girls were strong academically. Mandy was a member of the National Honor Society and a yearbook editor.

Mandy contacted Helen in her senior year to tell her that she would be working on her senior page and emphasized that she did not want to mess it up. Several months later, the yearbooks were printed and distributed to seniors first at a special senior event in May. Both Helen and Mandy were seniors. The day that the yearbooks were distributed, Helen discovered that there were several errors on her senior page. There was a picture of her that was distorted to make her look 40 to 50 lbs. overweight. The picture was shortened and stretched. Another picture contained a discoloration of one of her teeth. Helen's name was also misspelled in three places in the yearbook. The principal, Ms. Steadman, halted the distribution of yearbooks for ninth through eleventh graders while a full investigation was conducted. Several students who were on the yearbook staff were interviewed as were friends of Helen who claimed to have overheard comments made by Mandy. Ms. Mobay, the yearbook teacher, was also interviewed and was shocked by the distortions. She examined the pictures and stated that it looked as if the changes had been made on a computer.

Mandy initially denied that she had distorted the yearbook pictures on purpose, but later recanted after statements were shared by students who had overheard her making incriminating remarks. One student overheard Mandy say in an English class that Helen was the "fattest cheerleader at Morant Surrey High School and she was going to let everyone see that." Another student added that Mandy knew that Helen's name had

(Continued)

(Continued)

been misspelled. While conducting the investigation the School Resource Officer became involved, and once both parents were notified later that day, Helen's parents decided to press charges. Mandy's father was initially upset with the school administration and insisted that he be present if a school official talked to his daughter again. Shortly after meeting with the principal, Helen's parents also contacted the superintendent's office and the local television station. The parents were not critical of the school's handling of the situation, but they were very upset. The assistant superintendent directed Principal Steadman to stop yearbook distribution, start a full police investigation, and go through each page of the yearbook for any type of bias.

REFLECTIVE QUESTIONS

1. What consequences would you assign to Mandy? What rationale would you give for your decision?

2. How would you handle the publicity? What and how would you communicate to parents and the community?

3. What would you do to support Helen?

4. What would you communicate to faculty and staff?

5. How do you anticipate that this situation would affect seniors? Ninth through eleventh graders?

6. What would you do about yearbook distribution?

Turn to the Resources section in the back for a summary of how Ms. Steadman handled this case.

CASE STUDY #4

Cyberbullying

Dr. Howell, principal of Coventry Midlands High School, received an e-mail from Dr. and Mrs. Jasper in November. In the letter, the Jaspers stated that they believed that Dr. Howell was aware of a recent incident of harassment and bullying against their son, Martin, which they indicated was a violation of the school's policy code that prohibits discrimination, harassment, and bullying. A student named Sam created a Facebook group titled "We hate Martin" in which Sam stated, "I have decided we shall band together and create a force of hatred so strong he'll finally off himself." In addition, a second student named Dianne asked for and was granted administrator rights to the Facebook group, and she made statements such as "hopefully he will kill himself." Assuming that the principal was aware of these recent events, the Jaspers stated that they would like to know what disciplinary action had been or would be taken against Sam and Dianne. Mrs. Jasper added that when Dianne saw Martin at the mall over the weekend, she physically assaulted him. Mrs. Jasper stated that she and her husband had not decided whether or not to file assault charges against Dianne pending information about the school's plans for disciplinary action for the Facebook incident.

The Jaspers made Dr. Howell aware of a similar incident that occurred 6 months earlier in May of the previous school year while Martin was still a student at Coventry Midlands High School. The most recent incident was the impetus for contacting the principal. Midlands students posted a series of messages on Facebook encouraging Martin to commit suicide and took bets on if or when he would actually kill himself. As a direct result of that incident, Martin was hospitalized for over a week for treatment of severe depression. As part of his recovery from his depression, Martin was asked to make a plan regarding the best way to approach his schoolwork. He decided the best approach was to repeat eleventh grade in a high school without the hostile environment that had developed. Martin's request to transfer to another high school in the district, Surrey Glen High School, was granted. Dr. and Mrs. Jasper stated that since transferring to Surrey Glen where Martin was currently a student, Martin had been much happier in school. Martin worked hard to develop a strong network of close friends, and his grades were much better than they had been in years. Within days of Martin's hospitalization in late May of the previous school year, the Jaspers indicated that they had reported to the assistant principal, Ms. Gray, and the counselor, Mr. Brown, that Martin had been the victim of cyberbullying and harassment. The Jaspers asked if either Ms. Gray or Mr. Brown had created any written documentation and if so, they would like to request copies. When Dr. Howell communicated with the assistant principal, Ms. Gray stated that the majority of her conversations with the Jaspers centered on Martin's schedule and his request to drop Comparative Religions. Ms. Gray said that Mrs. Jasper had mentioned that Martin planned to transfer to another district high school and that he had been hospitalized, but Mrs. Jasper had not shared specific details about the reason for the hospitalization or the transfer. Mrs. Jasper, had, however, shared an e-mail about the Facebook account with Mr. Brown and added that she was considering contacting the parents of the other students. Mr. Brown had not shared that e-mail with Ms. Gray.

REFLECTIVE QUESTIONS

1. As the principal, what questions would you have for the assistant principal and counselor?

2. What do you know about the Facebook incident?

3. What would you like to know?

4. What consequences would you assign to Sam and Dianne?

5. What are the mitigating factors related to Facebook?

6. Who else would you involve in your investigation?

7. What would you say to Dr. and Mrs. Jasper?

8. What type of support would you offer to Martin?

9. What communication would you have with Martin's current principal at Surrey Glen High School?

Turn to the Resources section in the back for a summary of how Dr. Howell handled this case.

6

Decisions About Faculty and Staff

I believe as a principal the most important decision
I make is who to hire. I hire the best people, then I get out of the way.

Mr. Baron, Principal—Maryland

When asked about their most difficult decisions, 20 of the 21 principals interviewed mentioned faculty and staff evaluation issues. In this chapter, we discuss important decisions expert principals made to monitor classroom instruction by conducting regular classroom walkthroughs and observations. We also explore difficult evaluation decisions that include decisions to fire a popular coach, terminate an assistant principal, make budget cuts to teaching positions, and pursue the nonrenewal of teachers.

Before making the excruciating decision to fire or nonrenew a faculty or staff member, it is essential to first build the teacher community by making excellent hiring selections and establishing a trusting school environment so that evaluation decisions will not be misinterpreted. Several principals discussed their decisions to focus on nontenured teachers and provide teachers with ongoing constructive feedback and support, particularly in instances when significant instructional adjustments were needed.

Hiring the Best Staff

One of the best decisions any principal can make is to focus on hiring excellent staff. How do you do this? First, move quickly and begin the hiring process as soon as a principal learns that there is a vacancy from retirement or a resignation. Most districts have a comprehensive hiring process in place that includes traditional measures such as posting the position on the district website and participating in job fairs (if they still exist in your community). Well-connected principals also use informal networks at universities, other districts, churches, fellow principals, and administrators.

Second, as part of the interviewing process, it is advisable to include department chairs, grade-level leaders, and teachers on the hiring team and to jointly develop interview questions. The questions should be crafted to reveal content knowledge, passion, and organizational fit. Finally, leave time to check recent and current references, and if possible, invite the candidate to teach a lesson to students at your school. Many candidates can perform well in an interview but their self-presentation in an interview situation may not be indicative of their performance in a classroom.

While working as a principal, I was faced with a teacher vacancy after promoting a teacher on staff to a newly developed position. Since we were at the midyear point in the school year, I knew that we would not have the best candidate pool. When we found an experienced teacher from a well-respected public university who had experience teaching in a competitive neighboring district, we hired her. Unfortunately, though she interviewed well, she encountered significant classroom management issues in our highly diverse urban environment and demonstrated a negative attitude toward underachieving children. Fortunately, our district had a policy about hiring midyear teachers on a temporary expiring contract. She was not rehired the next school year. Hiring candidates during the traditional hiring season in the spring will likely yield better candidates. If there is a midyear resignation or retirement, if possible, consult Human Resources about the option of an expiring 1-year contract. Had we invited the candidate to teach a class, we would likely have anticipated her challenges with managing student discipline.

Creating a Caring School Environment

Hiring great staff is an important part of creating a positive school culture. But that is only the beginning. Principals face the challenge of integrating great new hires into a collegial, caring environment. Principal Baron (MD) stated, "From the custodians, I hired everyone based on their relational capacity. I don't know if this person can teach or not, but I can get a gauge on whether they can relate to kids. I can teach someone how to teach, I can't teach them how to care." Mr. Adams (NC) explained that teachers who prioritize relationships with students contribute to establishing a healthy school culture. This was the most important factor to Mr. Baron when he hired teachers.

For me, it was not necessarily the most important factor, but it was a critical component. I developed interview questions that included relationship building

> "If the teachers aren't happy, nobody's happy." Principal Adams (NC)

and scenarios. During the interview process, I was cognizant of the fact that for many students, if they have not developed a positive, mutually respectful relationship with a teacher, they will refuse to learn in that teacher's classroom.

Mr. Adams specified how he maintains a positive environment at his school:

> If the teachers aren't happy, nobody's happy. You can feel it when teachers aren't happy. You can sense a positive culture. Most of the stuff I do, I call community people and ask. They either do it for free or for a ridiculously low price. Every month, I do something (for my teachers) just because. I do it because I want them to know how much I appreciate them.

Mr. Adams said he conceived several ideas after attending a conference. The president of Google was speaking and talked about how having a healthy staff increased productivity. Mr. Adams obtained a wellness grant and bought $5,000 worth of fitness equipment that included two elliptical machines that teachers can use during their planning periods. He bragged that he now has several teachers who do not need to purchase a gym membership because of the fitness space. It is unlikely that students will be successful if teachers are miserable so it is worthwhile for principals to focus on creating an environment where teachers feel good about coming to work every day. Much like Teacher Appreciation Week, which is a time when principals create opportunities to celebrate teachers, that sentiment can be carried throughout the year. I stated in Chapter 2 that one of my core values is prioritizing relationships. When I make decisions, I endeavor to ensure that teachers feel cared for and respected. It is precisely in an environment of caring and respect that tough decisions should be made so that the principal's actions are not misconstrued as vindictive.

Tips to Follow Before Firing a Coach

- Assess your core values, the school's core values, and the core values of the coach. Is there a conflict?
- Is winning more important than treating players with dignity and respect?
- Do you have the political support of your superintendent, school board/school committee, and the community to fire the coach?
- Articulate your rationale for firing the coach, but depending on contractual obligations, this is for your information only. Don't share with the coach.
- Anticipate how your decision will be perceived by others.
- Do you feel so strongly about firing this coach that if he or she were rehired you would resign?
- If you have any ambivalence, then consider other options, such as temporary suspension, written letter of reprimand, and so on.
- Develop a plan for immediate communication with students, parents, and, if applicable, the media.
- Set aside time for individual and team parent meetings as well as student meetings.
- Be prepared for backlash in the local paper, in the student newspaper, at school committee/school board meetings, and on Facebook and other social media sites.
- If you still feel strongly that this is the best decision, proceed.

Firing a Popular Coach

The next sections include factors principals considered and the subsequent repercussions of their staffing decisions to fire a popular coach or to terminate an assistant principal. Administrative and coaching positions are a vital part of the school community. Making sure that the right people are hired for those roles is an important part of the principal's responsibility. Conversely, one of the most difficult decisions that a principal can make is the decision to fire a coach. Since the scope of the coach's job is school-wide, any student who has attended a game or who has been part of the team may feel connected to the coach. Some coaches have been in their roles for decades so relationships between student athletes and their parents can be extremely potent. Additionally, any decision related to a coach is public so that decision may draw media attention. The cost of keeping the coach has to far outweigh the political challenges a principal will have to navigate in the wake of a firing decision. How does a principal come to the conclusion to make such a decision?

Two expert principals shared their stories about their decisions to fire high-profile coaches. In the first instance, Principal Cadbury determined that what he valued and what was best for his students was far more important than having a team with a winning basketball record. The school's basketball coach was more concerned about winning than he was about the young men he was coaching. Coach Clyde was a bully, and he was also very confrontational with the players on his team. If players made a mistake, Coach Clyde yelled at them and degraded them. Coach Clyde's father, a legendary coach, was a very prominent figure in the community. He was a former professional athlete and had coached former Major League Soccer (MLS) players. It was very

> Coach Clyde was a bully, and he was also very confrontational with the players on his team. If players made a mistake, Coach Clyde yelled at them and degraded them.

difficult for Mr. Cadbury to reach the decision that Coach Clyde had to be removed. But he concluded that he could not be who he says he is as a principal and keep Coach Clyde.

In his reflection about how powerful Coach Clyde was politically, Mr. Cadbury shared that most coaching positions go to teachers first. Coach Clyde had never been a teacher yet he was given the position. Qualified teachers who were interested in coaching expressed that they were afraid to apply for the basketball coaching position. Finally, after coming to the realization that what was happening was not right, Mr. Cadbury dismissed Coach Clyde. Mr. Cadbury said he believed that the dismissal would send the right message about his expectations for how students were treated and about what he expected from a member of his staff. Ironically, Mr. Cadbury followed the central office guidelines that Coach Clyde's father had put in place about posting emergency coach positions and hired a replacement coach who was a teacher in his school. Mr. Cadbury experienced considerable backlash for his decision. "I paid for it politically.

A lot of people came from outside the building (to criticize me). I think we're better for it. We went to the second round of the playoffs (without him)." Mr. Cadbury added that he did not enter the decision blindly. He thought carefully about the costs politically, but more important, he thought about what his administration was about. Mr. Cadbury talked about the ease of making the right decision, but the difficulties ensued after the decision was made. Mr. Cadbury had to navigate the political repercussions from firing a powerful, politically connected coach.

The decision to fire a popular coach should not be arbitrary. The rationale should be clearly outlined and communicated to all constituents. Before considering firing Coach Clyde, Mr. Cadbury consulted central office administrators to inquire about whether he would be supported. Once he determined that he would be supported, he proceeded. Multiple scenarios or frames should be considered so that the principal is prepared to respond to disgruntled teachers, parents, students, and the media.

Principal Henry (NC) shared his experience firing his football coach. Mr. Bridge had been a coach and physical education teacher in his building. Mr. Henry mentioned that his decision was based on his desire to take the football program in a new direction. Mr. Bridge maintained his teaching job at the school. Mr. Henry wisely provided Coach Bridge with limited information about his rationale. He simply informed Coach Bridge that he would no longer retain his position as football coach because he wanted to take the football program in a new direction. Mr. Henry described the impact of his decision: "Firing my football coach. It was a lot bigger than I thought it was. It was probably the most excruciating thing. It was the most difficult time of my life personally and professionally."

Mr. Henry added that he knew what he wanted to do and did it but was unprepared for what came next. After he fired his football coach, several people contacted his wife and began texting her about who to hire as Coach Bridge's replacement. The decision to fire the coach was made before the holidays so during Christmas time, Mr. Henry was bombarded with calls and text messages. He described coming to the realization that football is as big in North Carolina as it is in Texas. Mr. Henry's school has been in existence for more than 50 years. Principal Henry described his school as having two worlds where students straddle an economic and class divide. Mr. Henry received a lot of pressure from his community to reverse his decision. When it became clear that he would not change his mind, he endured threatening and harassing phone calls.

Firing a popular coach is not the type of decision that should be made without considering the ramifications, including the community and school response and whether the principal has support from the superintendent and school board or school committee.

> If the school leader will not be supported by the superintendent and the school board/ school committee, be prepared to have to reverse the decision if enough countervailing political support is garnered.

It is also vital that the principal is prepared to dedicate a considerable amount of time to fielding phone calls and e-mails and meeting with disgruntled parents, students, faculty, staff, and the media. In both these cases, the principals, Mr. Cadbury and Mr. Henry, felt compelled to make the decision and believed that the decision had to be made. Both stated that the actual decision was not difficult. The difficulty took place after the decision was made.

Difficult Evaluation Decisions About Faculty and Staff: Factors to Consider

Utilize key problem-solving processes

Reflect on core values

Determine the human impact

Analyze the whole picture

Consult others

It is critical that the principal is certain that this is the right course of action so that when that decision is challenged, the school leader is confident and, though pressured, is able to withstand the pressure to reverse the decision. In these cases, the principals utilized all three key problem-solving processes: data, improvement, and stakeholder. They gathered and analyzed data about the coach's actions, identified constraints including district policy and legal implications, and planned their approach. They reviewed the long-term outlook of their decisions, willingly faced potential conflicts introduced by their decisions, and considered multiple stakeholder perspectives. Additionally they reflected on connections to their core values, assessed the impact on school culture, analyzed the big picture of how the coach fit into the school community, determined the effect on students and the school community, and consulted central office administrators. Similar factors were considered when contemplating the removal of an assistant principal.

Removing Recalcitrant Assistant Principals

It is critical that there is good chemistry between teachers and assistant principals. Assistant principals need to be able to build effective relationships and communicate well. While the administrator's role is a supervisory role, it is also a service role. Assistant principals need to approach the position with service to teachers in mind. Once the principal has established the vision for the school, it is important that the assistant principal is capable of helping move that vision forward and not moving in opposition to the vision.

Mr. Rollins (MD) described his experience removing an assistant principal who was undermining the environment that he was trying to create in his school. Though he liked Mr. Bassett, there were continual reports from faculty that Mr. Bassett was abrasive. It was Mr. Bassett's first year as an assistant principal, and Mr. Rollins's second year as principal. When Principal Rollins spoke to Mr. Bassett about teacher concerns, Mr. Bassett presented a completely different story claiming that he had several detractors who were trying to set him up so he would be unsuccessful. Principal Rollins noticed that Mr. Bassett's style was authoritative, and he often micromanaged others. Mr. Bassett gave staff orders and refused to provide teachers with an explanation for his decisions. Mr. Bassett was beginning to distance himself from the team. "One day, he lost his cool and jumped in a subordinate's face. He wasn't remorseful. It was an overreaction. I felt to keep him there was to undermine the whole administrative piece. He was put on administrative leave."

Assistant principals typically have contracts and are not generally eligible for tenure. Removal of an assistant principal must nonetheless follow district contractual guidelines. Part of the impetus for firing popular coaches was based on the negative impact on the development of the school environment. For similar reasons, principals also came to the decision to remove recalcitrant assistant principals. It is a tough but necessary decision to remove assistant principals who are functioning contrary to school culture.

> **Tips for Making Teacher Budget Cuts**
>
> - Review staffing and ensure that class size mandates, laws that govern the budget, and class size obligations are met.
> - For high schools, determine which classes with low enrollment can be eliminated without jeopardizing graduation requirements for seniors.
> - Review teacher certification as necessary if shifting classes means that teachers who do not typically teach a particular class could now be assigned to a new class.
> - Identify your core values and the school's mission and allocate discretionary funds accordingly.
> - Ensure that the cut does not place undue strain on any particular group of students, particularly lower achieving students.
> - Keep class sizes for lower achieving students as small as possible.
> - Follow teacher tenure laws regarding layoffs or nonrenewals and seek guidance from Human Resources.
> - Examine programs and determine how the elimination of one or more teaching positions will impact your school's ability to continue to offer a particular program (e.g., cutting a German teacher position could result in the elimination of the German program).
> - Develop and articulate a clear, well-thought-through rationale that is not arbitrary.

Cutting Teaching Positions

In addition to making decisions about hiring the best staff and creating a caring environment with effective coaches and administrators in place, principals also make critical decisions about how to spend money based on what is important to the school and what they value. When cuts are required, the cuts should be aligned with the school's mission and the programs that the school states that it will be offering. A school with a music and arts focus should ensure that cuts do not decimate the programs that are fundamental to the school's mission. As Principal Rollins (MD) noted, "The budget speaks to where your heart lies—where you spend your money and time. If a school says they are about excellence in education, but you look at their budget and they haven't funded anything about Advanced Placement courses . . ." For high schools, investing in the

Advanced Placement program is indicative of support for college preparatory education. Genuine support can be seen when it matters most—in how a principal spends time and resources. When tough decisions have to be made about what to fund, there are of course contractual obligations, class size mandates, and laws that govern the budget, but for the discretionary funds, we spend money based on what we value most. When I was an elementary principal, I used discretionary funds for my students who were below grade level. It was my belief that we would progress as a school when our lowest achieving students were academically successful. That is what I valued so that is how I directed our school's funding. Mr. Edwards (NC) has released seven teachers in the last 2 years for budgetary reasons. Mr. Edwards, an 11-year veteran principal, said he is a people person who cares deeply about how cuts impact members of his staff. He also acknowledged the political ramifications for cuts and being prepared to respond to parents, students, and other teachers who disagree with the cuts. Mr. Edwards stated that he finds ways to absorb a loss before he sends someone packing. He tries to find ways by shifting positions, if necessary. He may need to move a math teacher who is dual-certified in science. He examines data from course registrations so that he does not have a situation where he has cut a math teacher, then has math classes of 32 students. He acknowledges that the response to his decision can be emotional or difficult because it is not popular. He also prepares himself for some backlash from parents or teachers who do not support the cut. Mr. Edwards indicated that he made budget decisions based on what he valued—what was best for kids after carefully assessing the human impact, other options, and the impact on the school's master schedule. As a former principal who cares deeply about teachers and appreciates the life investment that many teachers put into work with children, I recognize that it is painstaking to have to cut a teaching position, particularly when the teacher is beloved and highly effective. The cuts should not be arbitrary so when the principal's decision is questioned, a clear, well-thought-through rationale can be articulated.

As some budgets get smaller and smaller, principals are often faced with the tough decision of which staff members to cut. It is particularly difficult when the decision cannot simply be made based on the school's values or the principal's values but must be made based on imposed laws such as tenure laws that stipulate "last hired, first fired." Ms. Cantrell (MA) stated, "You have to decide how do you cut and do the least harm. I try to think ahead so that when the question is presented to me and I have to make the decision and I don't have much time, I have my priorities in line."

Ms. Cantrell mentioned that when faced with a recent budget cut, she had to decide between two teachers, a Latino male, Mr. Santos, who had been at the school for 5 years and a White teacher, Ms. Robbins, who had been at the school for 12 years. Regarding Ms. Robbins's job, the school could have still functioned without that position. Mr. Santos, however, played an important role inspiring Latino students, and he had done a lot of work at the school with social justice. Ms. Cantrell described Mr. Santos as having a powerful effect on the school's culture. Ms. Cantrell was forced to cut Mr. Santos's position due to teacher tenure laws about "last hired." Cutting the position meant that there were no other Latino males on staff. Faculty and students were very unhappy about the decision not to renew Mr. Santos. He was well liked and well respected.

> "You have to decide how do you cut and do the least harm." Principal Cantrell (MA)

Ms. Cantrell identified another budgetary decision. She had a tenured teacher with a chronic illness. She did not eliminate the position, but she cut it back to a .7 FTE since the job did not need to be full time. The teacher was given working hours that allowed her to keep health benefits, but the teacher still decided to resign. Four other positions also had to be eliminated that school year.

These shared experiences illustrate the challenges that principals sometimes experience when they are forced to cut valuable positions, and it is not always possible to keep the best candidate in a position. There may also be times when principals are forced to cut positions of staff members who are experiencing difficult personal circumstances. Those are heart-wrenching decisions that affect a person's livelihood. It helps to gather as much data as possible so that the decision made is an informed decision and a compassionate decision. Be prepared for opposition from staff who may question the decision. Because the decision involves personnel, the details cannot be shared with other staff members. It is important to examine the impact of the decision on morale and anticipate the types of conversations that you will have with faculty and staff. Ms. Cantrell added that she deliberated about how to keep the core programming in place with the money and resources that she has.

When making budget decisions, these expert principals strived to make budgetary decisions that were connected to what they valued and what was important to their schools. They also considered the human impact of their decisions and anticipated concerns that could be raised by staff members, parents, or students. Sometimes their decisions were based on tenure law or central office guidelines. They gathered data, looked at the big picture, and determined how potential budget cuts would affect course enrollment.

Monitoring Classroom Instruction

Principals must also make another set of crucial decisions about instructional supervision. Instructional supervision as I describe it includes monitoring classroom instruction and collaborating with others to conduct intense evaluations of ineffective teachers with a focus on nontenured teachers. While engaging in instructional supervision and making decisions about teacher nonrenewal, principals should reflect on their core values, consider the school culture, determine the human impact, analyze the big picture, and consult others. Mr. Rollins (MD) spoke about the time he devotes to instructional leadership and supervision.

> How a principal spends his time. If he spends a lot of time dealing with suspensions and management, his heart is in the management of the school. About two years ago, I decided on Tuesdays, I shut myself down and I teach teachers how to teach four periods a day. I do formal and informal (observations).

It is not possible to be an effective principal without focusing some time on suspensions and management. A high school principal could literally spend his or her entire day every day focusing on discipline and management, so focusing on instruction becomes a choice that must be prioritized or there will never be time to observe instruction in the classroom. One of my core values is keeping the students' best interests in mind. Excellent instruction is in the best interest of students, so monitoring instruction became one of my priorities. To find time to monitor instruction, I decided to begin most days in the classroom. It was a bit easier to predict my mornings, at least the first 2 hours of the day. After lunch it could become impossible to spend time in classrooms, depending on the demands of the day. I also treated classroom observations and classroom walkthroughs like appointments. When I was in a

"How a principal spends his time. If he spends a lot of time dealing with suspensions and management, his heart is in the management of the school." Principal Rollins (MD)

classroom, unless there was a crisis, I had my radio turned down and asked not to be interrupted.

When conducting regular classroom walkthroughs, it quickly becomes apparent who the strongest teachers are, as well as the mediocre ones and the ones who need support and intense feedback about curriculum and instruction. Expert principals have a clear picture of what good instruction looks like. One of the decisions expert principals make is to monitor classroom instruction through regular classroom observations and classroom walkthroughs. Classroom walkthroughs can be defined as concise, nonevaluative, systematic classroom observations that include teacher feedback. Walkthroughs generally last 5 to 15 minutes.

Conducting Intense Evaluations of Ineffective Teachers

In the process of conducting classroom walkthroughs, expert principals assess their entire faculty and generate a list of ineffective teachers. The decision to evaluate four or more ineffective teachers in 1 year takes hours of observation time, pre- and postconferences, and carefully crafting the language in the evaluations so that the teacher realizes that the evaluation reflects unsatisfactory performance. The principal also has contractual deadlines to comply with, and if working in a union state, the principal should

> "My first year, my most difficult decision, I had a staff of 26, and I made the decision to evaluate out 12 of them. The decision was do I really want to change the school culture?" Principal Rodriguez (MA)

be prepared to meet with a union representative if requested to do so. Expert principals recognize that to move out ineffective teachers they must adhere closely to the district's evaluation system and meet all contractual deadlines. It only makes a school better to move out ineffective teachers; however, it is incredibly time-consuming to evaluate an ineffective teacher. Principal Rodriguez (MA) stated,

> My first year, my most difficult decision, I had a staff of 26, and I made the decision to evaluate out 12 of them. The decision was do I really want to change the school culture? They were all tenured, two were union reps. None of them went to arbitration. I put in all my energy. I was young, I did it my first year. All 12 of them went. The assistant headmaster decided to leave before I evaluated him. In my life, I have never been to arbitration for any of my evaluations.

Ms. Rodriguez faced extraordinary circumstances in her small urban high school that propelled her to make decisions about immediate staffing changes. The term *evaluate out* refers to engaging in an intense evaluation process that results in the nonrenewal or resignation of a poor or mediocre teacher. When I was a principal, I carefully scanned the landscape for poor or mediocre teachers and made sure that I focused on intense evaluations so that any poor or mediocre teachers on staff were evaluated out each year. I was not so ambitious as to evaluate out 12, but with a cadre of assistant principals also engaged in the same focused task, intense evaluations of at least two to three underperforming teachers per administrator per year should be feasible. The goal is not to target teachers who are performing well, but to provide clear, timely feedback to underperforming teachers and to ultimately maintain an excellent teaching staff. Evaluating out ineffective teachers will have a profound effect on school culture. Generally speaking, this is not the task to take on in the first year of a principalship unless extraordinary circumstances dictate that it is necessary.

The development of the teacher community should come first: it should be apparent that the principal cares about the school, the teachers and the students and is not simply there to dismantle the school. Part of the challenge of moving out ineffective teachers is the impact on culture. Once the process of moving out ineffective teachers begins, an environment of fear and mistrust can develop if the process is not managed properly. What the principal does not want is for good teachers to be fearful about the security of their jobs. After conducting an assessment of the school environment, it will become clear if changes should be made. When, how, and if the noted changes should be made will take careful consideration of timing, school culture, resources, well-articulated goals, support from central office, your teachers, and a host of other interrelated factors. (For additional information on introducing change, see Chapter 3.) In addition to reflecting on the core value of monitoring classroom instruction, considering how intense evaluations will affect the school culture, and assessing the impact on highly effective teachers, it is also important to consult others as part of the evaluation process.

Collaborating With Others on the Evaluation Process

In conjunction with a coach or an administrative team member, principals conduct intense evaluations which consist of weekly evaluations of ineffective teachers. Each principal needs to determine the number of intense evaluations that will be conducted based on district contractual obligations, the time available, and the number of qualified assistant principals or instructional coaches who can assist with the process. Typically instructional coaches do not conduct evaluative visits, but strong coaches can help the principal identify poor or mediocre teachers and can increase the number of visits to the classroom of an underperforming teacher. In addition to the required three to four annual evaluative visits, unscheduled weekly visits of underperforming teachers should be prioritized. In some states, there may be contractual limitations placed on the number of evaluative visits that can be conducted. It is important to review the district's evaluation requirements at the onset of the school year.

Dr. Manning (MA) is the principal of a large school with 150 faculty members. She has determined to prioritize teachers who are having difficulties who are in their first 3 years. She puts year-3 teachers on her evaluation list and visits their classrooms three times, once a month from September to November. Dr. Manning stated that she was currently in the process of nonrenewing a teacher, Mr. Healey. She acknowledged how hard decisions about nonrenewal can be because they involve an individual's livelihood and career. She tries to look at situations from the viewpoint of the students. She believes that her students deserve the best. Each time Dr. Manning visited Mr. Healey's class, she gave him specific feedback, and the program director also visited and gave Mr. Healey feedback.

Dr. Manning shared her observation of Mr. Healey's English 12 class, which was composed almost entirely of boys and predominantly non-White boys. She queried, "How do you have boys asleep when you are talking about James Baldwin? Nobody gave him feedback the previous two years." Dr. Manning admitted that Mr. Healey should have received feedback sooner, but added that he should have been working much harder to reach all his students. Dr. Manning decided to have a difficult conversation with Mr. Healey to prepare him for what she had to say because his performance was in the needs improvement category. Mr. Healey was shocked and disappointed. Dr. Manning mentioned that Mr. Healey's colleagues had begun to send her e-mail on his behalf and the union representative had also asked to meet with her about Mr. Healey. Dr. Manning expressed a readiness to meet with the union representative but added that she can listen, but she can't say anything about Mr. Healey's performance. Dr. Manning shared that she was very comfortable with her decision.

Concerned that she already has a lot of mediocre teachers, Dr. Manning indicated that she cannot afford to have another one.

Dr. Manning emphasized that for her to retain provisional teachers they have to be the best. She added that earlier in her career she let some ineffective teachers slip through the cracks and now they are tenured teachers. She notes that the most effective indicator of student achievement is teacher quality. She describes herself as being tougher now. There have been instances where she has encouraged ineffective tenured teachers toward retirement. She told them that basically they were not meeting the standards so they could proceed in one of two ways: termination or retirement. Most opted for retirement. Confronting a mediocre teacher requires facing conflict. No matter how clear a principal believes that he or she has been, the teacher is often surprised to receive very critical feedback. It is difficult in the short term, but in the long term, the decision to evaluate out an ineffective teacher is in the best interest of students and the school community. To complete the process successfully, principals should be meticulous about collecting data and following state personnel laws and district guidelines. It is helpful to have the input of a coach, assistant principal, or department chair. Even though the approach may have to be precipitous at times, the principal should always weigh the human impact and consider how other teachers may respond when they learn about the nonrenewal of a colleague. I always began the school year prioritizing nontenured teachers, especially those in the first 2 years of employment.

Prioritizing Nontenured Teachers

Several principals discussed their focus on nontenured teachers and their dedication to conducting classroom observations and meeting with teachers to give them verbal and written feedback. Principal Wallace (MD) described her decision to confront an ineffective nontenured English teacher, Mr. Hennigan, who was in his third year. In this case, there was very little evidence of planning and Mr. Hennigan did not take the time to develop an inviting environment in his classroom. In her first month as a principal, Ms. Wallace realized that Mr. Hennigan was not a good match for the school. Ms. Wallace visited Mr. Hennigan's classroom seven times and provided him with feedback about his performance. In a meeting with Mr. Hennigan about her expectations, Ms. Wallace asked him a pointed question: "Is this something that you really want to do?" Mr. Hennigan's students were clearly not learning. Within 2 days of meeting, Mr. Hennigan submitted his resignation and told Ms. Wallace that he could not live up to her expectations. One of the key problem-solving processes that expert principals utilize is an improvement focus where the principal faces the conflict and considers the long-term outlook. Principal Wallace was willing to face a conflict by confronting mediocrity in her teachers. It can be difficult to provide teachers with constructive feedback, particularly when significant instructional adjustments are needed. While monitoring instruction, the long-term outlook pertains to judgments about the current effectiveness of the teacher observed and whether that effectiveness will improve or diminish in the future. Once teachers become tenured, the school and district have made a long-term commitment. Principal Wallace also focused on data that supported her assertion about mediocrity.

In Maryland and Massachusetts, after completing 3 years of teaching, nontenured teachers are eligible for tenure. In 2013, the North Carolina State Legislature enacted a law ending teacher tenure. Over 50 North Carolina School Boards adopted resolutions opposing the law. After facing a lawsuit from two districts, the North Carolina Association of Educators, and a group of teachers, two judges separately struck down the law as unconstitutional. At present, the merits of the law are being debated as the Legislature contemplates an appeal (Brown, 2014). Before the law was established, in North Carolina, after completing 4 years, teachers became eligible for tenure. It is critical to determine how soon intense evaluations of nontenured teachers should begin. Generally speaking, it is advisable to conduct intense evaluations of nontenured teachers the first 2 years. As they move into the third year (depending on the number of years before teachers are eligible for tenure), teachers begin to think that their performance is effective and they may become less amenable to change. It is also vital to provide all teachers who are new to your building with regular, specific feedback about their performance during the first 2 years.

> Principal Manning (MA) acknowledged how hard decisions about nonrenewal can be because they involve an individual's livelihood and career. She tries to look at situations from the viewpoint of the students. She believes that her students deserve the best.

Mr. Peppers (NC) also focuses on the evaluation of nontenured teachers. Mr. Peppers added that this year, he decided to nonrenew an underperforming, uncommitted nontenured teacher with extensive absences who was rarely prepared when she came to work. The teacher was a first-year teacher on an expiring 1-year contract who filed for worker's compensation after claiming that she was injured while breaking up a fight. The claim was denied, but her absence left a class in a tested area with a substitute for over 2 months. In the long run, Mr. Peppers believes that the decision to remove the teacher was still a good decision. Fortunately this nonrenewal will be accomplished fairly easily because the teacher has a 1-year expiring contract. Dr. Manning and Mr. Peppers both noticed the mediocrity of their new nontenured teachers and opted to utilize key problem-solving processes. They focused on improvement and data.

It is important that teachers understand the principal's priorities and evaluations are not used as a "gotcha." When I was a principal, at the beginning of each year, I made sure that teachers had a copy of the teacher evaluation instrument, understood their rights and the evaluation process, and understood what I would be looking for during classroom observations. Are students engaged? Is time used effectively? Does the teacher create a safe and orderly classroom environment? Is the teacher knowledgeable about the content? Is there evidence of a well-planned lesson? Does the teacher engage students in critical thinking and problem solving? Does the teacher facilitate student learning and provide helpful feedback? Has the teacher created mutually respectful relationships with students?

Although high school principals may recognize good instruction, they are not usually knowledgeable about pacing and content in all their departments. It is difficult to be knowledgeable about German, Physics, Calculus, and World History. I provided written feedback within 10 days of a formal evaluative visit in accordance with contractual obligations. Following classroom walkthroughs, I shared written teacher feedback before I left the class. (See the Resources section for my favorite walkthrough instrument.)

Summary

Before deciding to conduct intense teacher evaluations, these expert principals determined whether retaining the teacher was in the best interest of students. Principals also considered state tenure laws and district polices regarding the nonrenewal process and timeline. In choosing to move forward with intense evaluations, principals examined the human impact and how the decision would affect the teacher and the rest of the school community. When a principal is developing documentation that may lead to nonrenewal, consultation with Human Resources is expected. Principals need to develop the school's evaluative focus and therefore decide which teachers they will intensely evaluate. Expert principals invest an inordinate amount of time conducting observations and providing feedback to nontenured teachers.

Chapter 6 Case Study

While the focus in this chapter is largely on nontenured teachers, it does not mean that ineffective tenured teachers should not be monitored. Evaluating out tenured teachers is a much more intricate and lengthy process that should include Human Resources and legal team involvement at the onset. Moving out an ineffective tenured teacher may take 2 or more years. When asked about their most difficult or complex decisions, 20 of the 21 principals interviewed mentioned staffing issues. Of the staffing issues that principals manage, the supervision of ineffective tenured teachers is likely the most difficult. As you read the following case study, consider, if you were the principal, how would you handle this situation?

CASE STUDY #5

Teacher Disregards District Policies

Mr. Owen, a tenured teacher, had been teaching English at Principal Zenga's school for 6 years. Mr. Owen was young, very personable, and well liked by students. Dr. Zenga had originally hired Mr. Owen to work at her affluent suburban high school in an effort to diversify her staff and bring more young men into the school. Dr. Zenga's major work was around the achievement gap, and Mr. Owen was a voice supporting that work. Mr. Owen's career at the school, however, had been less than stellar. Dr. Zenga described Mr. Owen as a mediocre teacher. Mr. Owen also had a pattern of arriving late and not putting in enough preparation time for class. The first time Mr. Owen had an issue, he was teaching a Shakespeare play and tried to act out a scene. During class, Mr. Owen asked one of his students if anyone had a knife. A student produced a pocket knife. Even though Mr. Owen was aware of student policy about weapons, he returned the knife to the student. Dr. Zenga met with Mr. Owen about the incident and appropriate action was taken.

Two years later, there was a broken desk in Mr. Owen's classroom. As students entered the classroom, Mr. Owen asked if any of the students had a screwdriver. A student said no, but she said that she had a Swiss Army knife. Mr. Owen let the student keep the Swiss Army knife while he walked the student to the assistant principal's office. Dr. Zenga expressed concerns that Mr. Owen was exercising poor judgment. While the student was in the assistant principal's office, the student was searched and the assistant principal found marijuana in the student's possession. The

(Continued)

(Continued)

parents of the student raised questions about the reason their daughter had been searched and questioned the school administration about any possible consequences. Dr. Zenga was becoming increasingly concerned about what Mr. Owen might do next and how his actions would impact students in her school.

A month after that second incident, Mr. Owen was conducting a review for a test. Mr. Owen required students who gave the wrong answer to a question to do pushups. One of the students who had an IEP (individualized education program) was required to do over 40 pushups. The parent of the child complained vehemently about how her daughter had been treated and threatened to pursue legal action. Dr. Zenga deliberated about whom else to consult about the incidents with Mr. Owen. A month later, Mr. Owen showed a DVD with graphic sexual content in one of his classes. Dr. Zenga had some crucial decisions to make about students, her communication with parents, and the performance of Mr. Owen.

REFLECTIVE QUESTIONS

Summarize what you know about the incidents with Mr. Owen and the students. What would you like to know?

1. Should disciplinary consequences be assigned to the students in both cases? If so, what consequences would you assign to the student for each incident?

2. Should disciplinary consequences be assigned to Mr. Owen for each incident? If so, what consequences would you give?

3. Did the parents who had concerns about searching their daughter have legitimate concerns?

4. What is your assessment of the decision to require students to complete pushups as a consequence for giving an incorrect answer?

5. What should be communicated to the parents of the students and to Mr. Owen's students?

6. In a union state, what particular issues need to be addressed when communicating with a tenured teacher about concerns?

7. What steps should be taken and who else needs to be informed about the incidents?

8. How would you respond to parents about the inappropriate DVD?

Turn to the Resources section in the back for a summary of how Dr. Zenga handled this case.

7

Decisions About Practices, Policies, and Programs

My first year as an administrator, transcripts were fraudulent. It made the news. It was really ugly.

Ms. Wallace, Principal—Maryland

Principals are faced with making arduous decisions about practices, policies, and programs. In this chapter, expert principals share their decisions to confront duplicitous faculty practices, manage allegations of faculty misconduct, supervise faculty mediation, transform schedules, and negotiate with the central office about decisions pertaining to practices, policies, and programs. As principals addressed these multifaceted infractions and programmatic concerns, they utilized key problem-solving practices outlined by Brenninkmeyer and Spillane (2008), which include a data focus, an improvement focus, and a stakeholder focus. Principals engaged in a rigorous process of investigation (data focus) before reaching any conclusions. Human Resources was also consulted along with the district's employee handbook to determine what staff action should be taken (stakeholder focus) and what violations may have transpired. As a solution was devised, principals considered how the school would be improved over the long term (improvement focus).

Uncovering Duplicitous Faculty Practices

One of the most difficult decisions a principal can face is addressing duplicitous faculty behavior. We will review practices that include fraudulent transcripts, the unauthorized use of the school building, and decisions principals made to curtail these behaviors.

Fraudulent Transcripts

Ms. Wallace (MD) divulged her experience as a first-year principal and her courageous decision to implement significant changes. While reviewing her school's master schedule, Ms. Wallace was disturbed by her discovery of glaring errors that included nonexistent classes and student transcripts with grossly inaccurate information. Ms. Wallace met with staff members to determine if there were any legitimate alternative explanations based on her findings.

> Students needed classes for graduation that they were promised. Fictitious classes were developed, and guidance counselors and noncertificated people were in those areas. It was a huge concern, and classes that needed to be there weren't. I said I need to have the master schedule to see if my seniors had what they needed. People went on FMLA (Family and Medical Leave Act) the next day. I couldn't sleep. I had to review things to make sure that my facts were right.

It soon became apparent, however, that the missing or distorted information could only be explained by fraud. Many of those responsible chose to take a leave of absence rather than respond to the improprieties that were exposed. Once Ms. Wallace's suspicions were validated, she conferred with her superintendent about what would be communicated to faculty, students, parents, and the media and the resolutions that would be developed.

As a first-year principal wondering what my future was, I immediately reported it to the superintendent. He sent in a team to help students get what they needed, evening classes, Sunday classes. They had to get the hours done. We lived in this building. There were some tough conversations with parents and the community, ducking and dodging news reporters. Some of the parents were angry. It gave the teachers a sense of hope. They knew it was going on, but didn't know what to do. They thanked me for bringing it to light.

Decisions About Practices, Policies, and Programs: Factors to Consider

Utilize key problem-solving processes

Reflect on core values

Consider school culture

Determine the human impact

Analyze the whole picture

Consult others

In addition to utilizing key problem-solving processes, as principals made decisions about duplicitous faculty practices they were also influenced by core values and school culture. Principals also considered the human impact of their decisions, the whole picture, and whether to consult others. As they confronted faculty practices which included exposing fraudulent transcripts and embezzlement, principals were driven by their core values. For Principal Wallace those core values included acting in the best interest of her students and maintaining her integrity. Principal Rodriguez questioned whether allowing a rogue coach to conduct business for personal gain benefited students in her school. The answer was a resounding no. As an integral part of their decision making, these principals were compelled to radically transform a school culture that promulgated this type of deviant faculty behavior. Given the nature of the violations, both principals needed to quickly become students of the culture in their schools as they introduced the changes. At the forefront of their decision making was determining how students and their faculty would be impacted. These were both very complex and very difficult decisions.

As they reviewed the whole picture, the principals fastidiously assessed the foreground and background of the dilemma. They also identified the core problem and made decisions to expand their field of attention by considering policy and legal implications and visualizing potential solutions to the impending crisis.

Unauthorized Use of the School Building

After accepting a principalship at an underperforming urban school where unscrupulous behavior had been allowed to continue unchecked for years, Ms. Rodriguez (MA) made the decision to fire a very popular coach. Ms. Rodriguez's charge was to turn around the school in 2 years so she had support from the superintendent to make radical changes. The coach, Mr. Alban, had been permitting students and outside groups to use the school building without providing payment to the school. Students and community members were charged for using the school facilities, but Mr. Alban profited from the payments. Ms. Rodriguez added, "He thought he was running his own business here. After doing the investigation, I had to give him a trespass notice and fire him. It needed to be done. He had been doing it for many years."

It would have been easier to ignore the perfidious behavior since it had been going on for years, but Ms. Rodriguez chose to interrupt the behavior and regain control of her school. After making her decision, Ms. Rodriguez had to respond to student complaints and complaints from suburban community members who had been utilizing the space. Her car was also vandalized. There was a cost to Ms. Rodriguez personally for the decisions that she made.

> It would have been easier to ignore the perfidious behavior since it had been going on for years, but Ms. Rodriguez chose to interrupt the behavior and regain control of her school.

Both of these expert principals conducted an extensive process of data gathering before concluding that faculty members had engaged in duplicitous behavior. All other rival explanations were explored. District policy governing faculty behavior was reviewed, and Human Resources advice was also sought. In addition to handling cases of duplicitous faculty practices, principals made decisions to consult with the central office about the impact of policies, which included filing a child abuse report, managing allegations of faculty misconduct, and supervising faculty mediation.

Policy: The Impact of Central Office on Leadership Decision Making

The U.S. Department of Health and Human Services, Child Welfare Information Gateway (2012) report indicates that 48 states have requirements for professions that are obligated to report child abuse and neglect. In some states, that report is referred to as a 51A.

Two principals, one from North Carolina and one from Massachusetts, recalled their experiences adhering to district policy by filing a 51A against a teacher in their building. In each of the subsequent cases involving misconduct and mediation, principals consulted the central office about their decisions. Ms. Lyons (NC) communicated her experience investigating a charge made by a student against one of her staff members. School board policy required her to involve Human Resources and law enforcement. It was extremely difficult because she was not allowed to communicate details to her staff, parents, or students. A criminal investigation ensued. Ms. Lyons shared that she was ordered not to say anything to her staff, but her staff spent a great deal of time requesting meetings and asking questions about the incident. Ms. Lyons acknowledged the impact of the allegations on the career of the accused staff member but quickly added that her priority was making sure that her students were safe. "The waiting time for the investigation. It was stressful, not knowing the outcome. In the meantime, you had to continue business as usual and the kids asking questions: You cannot go into detail." Ms. Lyons's investigation influenced her decision about how to proceed. Conducting a thorough investigation was vital to ensure that the child was not placed in a situation that was unsafe. It was also very important to have documentation to support the decision and to make sure that guidance and support were solicited from the central office, district attorneys, and law enforcement.

Ms. Lily (MA) explained, "I had to file this 51A because there was an accusation of abuse. Although I did my own internal investigation and didn't find any proof, the district policy was if there is any allegation substantiated or not—if you have reasonable belief—you should call." Ms. Lily believed that the decision making was being taken away from the principal. She noted that other principals in similar situations had not filed a 51A in the past. She expressed concerns about the protection for teachers against false accusations. Though she was obligated to report the alleged abuse and she followed district guidelines, she believed that doing so went against her core philosophy. Ms. Lily anticipated the affect that a false accusation of abuse would have on the school community. She wrestled with the dilemma of how to support teachers while reassuring students and families that she was prioritizing their protection. "I knew the impact that would have for the community. It is very challenging to balance these two seemingly contradictory expectations." Both principals who filed a 51A mentioned the considerable amount of time spent meeting with teachers, students, and families. When addressing an allegation that requires filing a report of abuse or neglect, confidentiality is an expectation. The allegations should be addressed without reporting details to faculty that violate privacy laws. The teacher that is the subject of the investigation can share details with colleagues, but there is very little that the principal can communicate. The primary factors considered in addressing this type of decision included focusing on data, the human impact, consulting others (Human Resources), and assessing school culture. Ultimately, district policy that was enforced by the central office precluded any decision making at the building level. While the principal managed the outcomes of decisions at the building level, laws and district policy governed the principal's actions.

Managing Allegations of Faculty Misconduct

While I was working as a school administrator, I investigated an incident of an alleged sexual relationship between a staff member and a student. I received a call from Ms. Merryfield, the parent of one of my female students, Pamela. Ms. Merryfield claimed that two girls had reported that Pamela told them that she was having sex with a teacher. Ms. Merryfield did not have the name of the teacher, but mentioned that a teacher had brought Pamela home a couple of times. I followed district policy, which required me to contact school police and report the information. As a mandated reporter, I also contacted the Department of Social Services. I was advised not to communicate directly with Pamela, but to also contact the police Sexual Assault Unit that day.

> Shakeshaft (2013) shares external inhibitors that can prevent abuse, "Good policies and procedures, annual training, clarity about boundaries, parent awareness, and staff vigilance—these all work to minimize abuse."

I communicated with Detective Brandy from the Sexual Assault Unit, and she informed me that she would contact Ms. Merryfield to conduct an investigation. When I followed up with Detective Brandy, she indicated that she had called Ms. Merryfield a couple of times, but Ms. Merryfield was hesitant to file a police report because she had not heard the information directly from Pamela. Detective Brandy did not communicate with Pamela about the alleged incident. After investigating, Detective Brandy informed me that because Pamela was 17 years old, there was nothing else that she could do. If Pamela consented, a crime may not have been committed. If Pamela were younger, it would be different since students 15 and under cannot consent. I asked Detective Brandy if I could talk to Pamela about the incident since about 2 weeks had passed since I made the report. I was told that at this juncture, I should handle the matter with the school district. I contacted Human Resources; my superintendent and I also contacted the district legal unit and spoke with the attorney. I was advised to talk to Pamela and try to prompt her to talk about the incident. The attorney was concerned about what steps could be taken if Pamela would not talk about the incident. When I met with Pamela, I shared with her the conversation I had with her mother, Ms. Merryfield, the steps I had taken in contacting the Sexual Assault Unit, and explained the reason I had not spoken with her sooner about the allegations. I also asked a counselor to be part of the meeting with Pamela. Pamela vehemently denied having a sexual relationship with a teacher. She insisted, "It hasn't happened. Girls talk. I'm never even home to talk to girls. I've never said nothing like that. I know what comes out of my mouth. I didn't do nothing like that. It never happened. No, no, no, no."

After school on the same day, Mr. Clover, a male staff member, asked to meet with me. He told me that Pamela had approached him during lunch and said that I talked to her about a teacher making a sexual advance toward her and that his name was mentioned. I had not mentioned any names to Pamela. Mr. Clover described the nature of his relationship with Pamela. He said that he had driven her home once. He said that Pamela is often in his office before school but with the door open. At times, another male staff person is present. He said he has had numerous conversations about how Pamela is doing in school, the type of company she keeps, and her future plans. Mr. Clover also mentioned that he had heard about the rumor about the two of them 3 to 4 weeks ago and mentioned two boys by name who he thought were connected to starting the rumor at school. I asked Mr. Clover directly if he had an inappropriate sexual relationship with Pamela at any time. He claimed that he had not. The district's attorney had advised me to meet with Mr. Clover and inform

Tips for Managing Claims of Faculty Sexual Misconduct

- Gather details from the person reporting the misconduct.
- Immediately report the misconduct to Human Resources, law enforcement, and the school district attorney.
- After receiving advice on how to proceed, conduct interviews as allowed and gather additional data. Only speak with those persons who are potential witnesses.
- Keep in mind the rights of the accused faculty member and strictly adhere to personnel guidelines. Obtain a statement from the accused faculty member. Avoid making accusations.
- Obtain a statement from the victim about the alleged misconduct.
- Notify the parent(s) of the alleged victim about the allegations.
- Follow up with the person reporting the misconduct and assure the person that you are taking steps to investigate.
- Do not provide the person with the results of your investigation. Encourage the reporting person to speak with law enforcement about next steps.
- If charges are filed, Human Resources will provide you with stringent guidelines about how to proceed. Do not deviate from those steps.
- Review school policies in place and determine if sufficient safeguards are in place to prevent abuse from occurring.
- Consult Human Resources before revising policies.

him that I did not have any proof; however, inappropriate sexual relationships with students would be not tolerated and if I obtained any proof, he would be disciplined.

I met with Pamela again and told her that she could feel free to speak with me or her counselor at any time if she had any information that she wanted to share. Pamela did not provide any further details about this incident. After my investigation, I questioned if an inappropriate relationship had occurred between Pamela and Mr. Clover. Since Pamela was unwilling to admit whether such a relationship took place, however, and no one had actually witnessed any inappropriate behavior, no further action could be taken since the only evidence was hearsay. Policy was followed and closure obtained, but there was no clear resolution.

Keeping law and district policies in the forefront, I was compelled to conduct an investigation into staff behavior and explore the possibility of misconduct. Therefore the problem-solving strategy I used included a data focus. I made the decision to follow laws to preserve confidentiality and to ensure faculty due process was followed. I also made pertinent decisions to communicate with law enforcement and Human Resources. Confidentiality was compromised, however, when students began to spread rumors about an inappropriate relationship between the teacher and the student. The human impact is a primary consideration when addressing decisions about misconduct or abuse allegations. Inevitably, the school community is affected so a stakeholder focus was prominent. Although the school community cannot be consulted, examining the whole picture by considering how the school may be affected is vital.

> Shakeshaft (2013) shares external inhibitors that can prevent abuse: Good policies and procedures, annual training, clarity about boundaries, parent awareness, and staff vigilance— these all work to minimize abuse. Knowing that other teachers and personnel will report inappropriate or questionable behavior also can inhibit an adult from inappropriate behavior with students (p. 11).

When this situation developed, I questioned the extent to which we had implemented sufficient safeguards to protect students from questionable behavior. When the allegations surfaced, I reviewed the processes for prevention of any potential or future abuse of children in our building. I reassured Pamela's mother that we were implementing external inhibitors to protect all our students from potential abuse. When making decisions about allegations of sexual misconduct, I utilized the data focus problem-solving process. I also analyzed the whole picture by assessing all details and consulted others, namely Human Resources, the attorney, and law enforcement.

Communicating With Human Resources About Faculty Mediation

Communicating with the Human Resources department about hostile faculty interactions is advisable. While principals may desire to protect faculty from adverse documentation in their personnel files, in some cases, Human Resources can provide valuable advice on how to navigate policies and procedures. Ms. Langely (MA) described a series of negative interactions that took place between a department chair and a faculty member in her building. The interactions led to required disciplinary personnel action. A faculty member was sharing information about a course at a department meeting and did not understand why an approval was not granted. Rather than meeting with the department head privately, the faculty member sent out an e-mail to the entire department and at a Professional Learning Community (PLC) meeting, the faculty member verbally attacked the department chair. Other faculty members in the department expressed that they felt uncomfortable during the exchange. Ms. Langley stated, "The department chair decided that this was insubordinate which is a pretty loaded term. This faculty member is incredibly talented, but incredibly arrogant."

Ms. Langely scheduled meetings on five separate occasions over a 2.5-week period in an attempt to resolve the matter. Ms. Langely tried to mediate the conflict between the department chair and the teacher to avoid personnel action. The union representative was invited to attend a meeting, but tempers flared and initially a resolution was not reached. When Ms. Langely communicated with Human Resources to notify them that she had been able to resolve the matter, she was chastised for not consulting them sooner and informed that a letter of expectation would need to be drafted and placed in the teacher's file. Ms. Langely shared her critique of the Human Resources office: "It's a different mindset, they have a very narrow interpretation of **Weingarten rights** and we have a difficult union. What they don't understand is it is more complicated at the high school." Weingarten rights include the right to have a union representative attend an investigatory interview. Ms. Langely was disappointed by the lack of support from the central office and by the lack of understanding about the nuances she faced as she tried to resolve the matter at her school. Ms. Langely did not deserve to be verbally berated by a central office member, but she also recognized that she should have notified Human Resources before scheduling multiple meetings to resolve the matter.

While it would appear that the principal should be able to mediate conflicts between faculty, if the conflict is not resolved and outsiders become involved (i.e., union representatives), Human Resources may require written documentation to be completed. Before communicating with faculty members to address a conflict, principals should be aware of district policies regarding mediation and conflict resolution.

Programs: The Challenge of Changes to the Master Schedule

At this juncture, we have reviewed how principals have handled decisions about practices and policies and their communication with the central office. In the following sections, we discuss decisions

Tips for Making Decisions About Practices, Policies, and Programs

- Consider the human impact of your decisions and conduct a thorough investigation that ensures that the rights of all involved parties protected.
- Even when pressed to do otherwise, strictly adhere to confidentiality. Law enforcement and central office should be consulted and school board/school committee policy and state laws should be followed closely.
- Pay attention to nurturing faculty who experienced feelings of alienation or who questioned whether they and other teachers were supported.
- Inform students and parents about how seriously administration is treating the allegations and make assurances about how students will remain safe.
- Given the legality and impact of policy, recognize that although you conducted the investigation and were in direct communication with students, parents, and teachers, ultimately, decisions about consequences for alleged abuse will not be decided by you.

principals made to programmatic changes in the master schedule. There are a few areas that profoundly affect how teachers teach: their classrooms, what they teach, and the schedule or when they teach. Certainly there are other areas, but these three areas in particular if changed will invoke in some cases visceral reactions from teachers. Some master schedule changes may be minor, but a bell schedule change is significant. A bell schedule change should only be tackled by an experienced principal who has established trust in the school. Central office support and advice should also be secured.

The three principals from Massachusetts and Maryland quoted in this section followed district policies as they made decisions to propose schedule changes that impacted budgets, staffing, and instructional time. Following district procedures does not guarantee the best outcome for the community; in one case, parent advocacy resulted in an overturned decision and a more amenable resolution. These principals acknowledged the importance of proceeding very slowly with major master schedule changes, soliciting lots of feedback, giving teachers opportunities to visit other schools and to meet with them in small groups. Principals also communicated with the central office about the proposed scheduling changes, anticipated resistance, and were prepared to alter the introduced changes if needed.

Eliminating a Language Program

Ms. Perez (MA) initially felt compelled to eliminate the Chinese language program at her school based on low enrollment and budgetary considerations. She was cognizant of the fact that many of the students who were taking Chinese were of Chinese descent and that about 50 students would no longer be able to take Chinese. Ms. Perez mentioned, "The decision to cut the Chinese program. The teacher had half the number of students of any other teachers in any other language." The decision was not well received by the Chinese community. Ms. Perez was concerned that for many students' parents there was a culture and language barrier that made it more difficult to ensure that the decision was communicated effectively. Fortunately the district decided it would provide the additional funds needed for the program. Although Ms. Perez followed the district process for program reduction, she was put in the difficult position of making an unpopular decision that was then reversed. When faced with a decision to eliminate an underenrolled program that serves a vocal minority, after exhausting all alternatives, it is advisable to enlist the support of parents who can articulate the adverse effects of the proposed changes. Central office may be able to identify alternate funding sources.

Ms. Perez also reflected on other experiences involving the central office and commented on the multitude of requests made by the district that she described as interfering with student learning. While she adheres to district policy, she does not do so without first assessing the request and considering the impact on her students and her school. "If they ask me to do something that will benefit my students, I'll do it immediately. If not, I'll just wait and they just send a reminder. I make judgment calls on how important (the request is)." At times, Ms. Perez will question or delay a response or offer an alternative that better meets the needs of her students. Ms. Perez is an experienced and well-respected principal; however, this strategy may not work in all situations and in all districts. In most cases principals should work harmoniously with the central office, but they should not be afraid to introduce counterarguments or challenges when proposed changes are detrimental or incongruous.

Master Schedule Formats

Before discussing the decisions that two principals made to introduce significant master schedule changes, an overview of master schedule formats is provided here. Zelkowski (2010) presented a brief overview of four common types of school scheduling formats: traditional, block, alternating block or the A/B block, and the Copernican block schedule. For traditional period schedules, students meet for year-long classes, which typically meet for 50 to 55 minutes a day for seven or eight periods a day. The most common block schedule is a 4 × 4, meaning that students have four 80- to 90-minute classes that meet for one semester. Table 7.1 is an example of a typical 4 × 4 block schedule. Variations of a typical block schedule are described below.

Table 7.1   4 × 4 Block Schedule

Period	Bell	Bell
1st Period	7:25	8:50
2nd Period	8:56	10:22
Lunch (A and B Lunch)	10:22	11:22
3rd Period	11:22	12:47
4th Period	12:53	2:18

The alternating block or A/B block schedule classes meet for a full year on an alternating schedule for 80 to 90 minutes. B block classes might meet on Monday, Wednesday, and Friday the first week, while A block classes meet on Tuesday and Thursday of the first week. For the following week, B block classes would meet on Tuesday and Thursday and A block classes would meet on Monday, Wednesday, and Friday.

For the less commonly used Copernican block schedule, there is one 4-hour block, then two or three 1.5-hour blocks. Each month, the schedule rotates between the 4-hour and 1.5-hour blocks. Alternately, a Copernican block schedule can also consist of two 2-hour blocks that rotate every 2 months and two or three 1.5-hour blocks.

Changing the Bell Schedule

Mr. Bliden (MA) described his decision to introduce a change in the bell schedule at his large suburban high school. Mr. Bliden's school currently has a traditional 8-day rotating schedule that does not allow for hiring part-timers, creates restrictions on space, and does not allow students to come early or leave late. It also has an on-site

Table 7.2 Current Bell Schedule

Regular Release	Early Release	X Block	Day 1	Day 2	Day 3	Day 4	Day 5	Day 6	Day 7	Day 8
7:25 → 7:30	7:25 → 7:30	7:25 → 7:30	HR	HR	HR	HR	HR	HR	HR	HR
7:34 → 8:21	7:34 → 8:08	7:34 → 8:10	A	H	G	F	E	D	C	B
8:25 → 9:12	8:12 → 8:45	8:14 → 8:51	B	A	H	G	F	E	D	C
9:16 → 10:03	8:49 → 9:23	8:55 → 9:32	C	B	A	H	G	F	E	D
10:07 → 10:54	9:27 → 10:00	9:36 → 10:13	D	C	B	A	H	G	F	E
		10:17 → 10:54								

112

	Regular Release	Early Release	X Block	Day 1	Day 2	Day 3	Day 4	Day 5	Day 6	Day 7	Day 8
	10:54 → 12:19 LUNCH	10:04 → 10:38	10:54 → 12:19 LUNCH	E	D	C	B	A	H	G	F
	12:23 → 1:10	10:42 → 11:15	12:23 → 1:10	F	E	D	C	B	A	H	G
	1:14 → 2:02	11:15 → 12:42 LUNCH	1:14 → 2:02	G	F	E	D	C	B	A	H
Drop Block				H	G	F	E	D	C	B	A

REGULAR SCHEDULE AND X BLOCK LUNCH

1st Lunch
Lunch: 10:54–11:24
Class: 11:28–12:19

2nd Lunch (split class)
Class: 10:58–11:22
Lunch: 11:22–11:52
Class: 11:52–12:19

3rd Lunch
Class: 10:58–11:49
Lunch: 11:49–12:19

EARLY RELEASE WEDNESDAYS' LUNCH

1st Lunch
Lunch: 11:15–11:45
Class: 11:49–12:40

2nd Lunch (split class)
Class: 11:19–11:43
Lunch: 11:43–12:13
Class: 12:13–12:42

3rd Lunch
Class: 11:19–12:10
Lunch: 12:10–12:42

preschool program, but it cannot do any crossover programming with the preschool because of the schedule. The high school is in the process, however, of introducing an early childhood education class.

Mr. Bliden indicated, "I have two options on the table. One will satisfy the majority of people, but will really upset the most vocal minority. There is an excitable or committed group that feels it is not the best schedule for their discipline." The schedules that were being considered were a major departure from the current schedule. The school was contemplating an option of going to a 6 x 8 with a rotating block in the afternoon. Mr. Bliden's school currently has a 7 x 8 schedule that has been in place for 15 to 20 years with fully rotating morning and afternoon blocks. Each of the seven daily periods meets for 47 minutes with an 8-day cycle.

The proposed schedule would have fewer class meetings, which is one of the primary reasons that the Math department expressed opposition to the plan. As Mr. Bliden began introducing the bell schedule options, it quickly became evident how difficult a bell schedule change would be for his faculty. After hearing that the Math and Science departments were unhappy with the proposed scheduling changes, Mr. Bliden conducted Math and Science department lunch meetings. Mr. Bliden emphasized that the primary purpose of the meetings was to listen to teachers, but Mr. Bliden also emphasized that though some changes were proposed, the exact format of the new schedule had not been predetermined. Faculty would have the opportunity to give input on several models.

> "I have two options on the table. One will satisfy the majority of people, but will really upset the most vocal minority. There is an excitable or committed group that feels it is not the best schedule for their discipline." Principal Bliden (MA)

Some faculty members personalized the move to a new schedule and expressed that they believe that Mr. Bliden had personally let them down. Mr. Bliden added, "The bell schedule has been the most difficult thing. It will keep me up at night. I worry that one teacher I would count as a friend won't be able to forgive me for changing the schedule." Ultimately, Mr. Bliden would like a schedule in place that is in the best interest of the students. Mr. Bliden acknowledged how hard the past couple of years have been for teachers given the advent of Common Core and a new teacher evaluation system. Stating that the demands of teachers are really different, Mr. Bliden elected to compromise for 1 year, classes that were 10 minutes longer (57 minutes) for the upcoming school year with time built in for professional development and for lots of departmental and school-wide discussions about the schedule. The school already spent the previous year developing the scheduling options that were presented to the faculty. Mr. Bliden indicated that his priorities moving forward into the pre-implementation stage were to move toward a schedule that all faculty could agree with and support. He believed that the level of upset would recede if he sent faculty to visit other schools, ask questions, and share their findings with the rest of the faculty. Growth is also spurring the change. A new schedule could help alleviate overcrowding, but Mr. Bliden is taking his time to carefully lead this effort. He has had about 2 years so far, and he will have one pre-implementation year to reach consensus.

Tips for Introducing Bell Schedule Changes

- Articulate the rationale for considering a bell schedule change.
- Include the pros and cons of current schedule.
- Conduct extensive research on alternative schedules.
- Communicate with central office and elicit support and advice.
- Decide how the decision will be made. Will it be consensus or voting (not recommended) or will you solicit advice from the faculty and make the final decision?
- Present two to three options to faculty in small-group and large-group meetings.
- Anticipate irrational opposition from teachers, students, and parents.
- Incorporate feedback in revised schedule proposal.
- If plausible, visit other schools and meet with their faculty.
- Decide which schedule you will support.
- Share revised proposal.
- Establish a timeline for implementation (1–2 years).

Introducing a Trimester Schedule

Ms. Wallace (MD) recounted her experience leading a change in the master schedule at her urban alternative high school. When she first arrived as principal, she prioritized meeting individually with all the students at her small high school. She scheduled 15-minute meetings with each of them. When she asked her students what did not work, one of the areas that students mentioned was the schedule. As students shared other experiences, Ms. Wallace recalled that as an alternative learner herself, she identified with their challenges. "I remember saying the same words and feeling those same thoughts." Ms. Wallace believed that although she was leading an alternative high school, her school followed a semester schedule, which is more conducive to a traditional high school. "I called my supervisor and asked to change our schedule to a trimester. To a lot of people, it appeared that I was giving students something. It meant accelerating instruction and grading." A trimester schedule allows students to take more courses during the school year. This is a benefit for alternative learners who may have more credits to make up in a year given previous experiences with course failure.

Ms. Wallace recalled having to sell the idea of a trimester schedule to her team so that they would be supportive of the change. The change influenced how guidance counselors worked with students and how quickly students could complete courses. Students are offered online credit recovery, but night school is not generally an option. Ms. Wallace also reflected on how the schedule change once adopted had vastly improved the school. "When I first came here, I had eight seniors. Now I have 45. I felt that was a difficult decision. I was going against all odds. I didn't know if it was going to be a disaster. I tapped into my high school experience. I couldn't sit in a class for hours and be lectured to." Ms. Wallace remarked that her students are excited about learning again. Most of the staff were supportive of the change, but Ms. Wallace is still working with others who, she states, do not solidly understand the concept of alternative education. Myers (2008) concurs about the importance of implementing a schedule change with the goal of improving learning for students: "All children truly can learn if educators across the country have the courage to examine ineffective past practices and realign time and support in a way that ensures success (p. 23)."

Both Mr. Bliden and Ms. Wallace were fully aware of the need to focus on key problem-solving processes as they moved forward with decisions to change the schedule. They invested a significant amount of time focusing on data by researching options. They focused on stakeholders by meeting with teachers, listening to the feedback, and making adjustments based on that feedback. They both believed that their introduction of a new schedule would result in an improvement for students (improvement focus). Additionally, both principals considered their school's culture, the human impact of the proposed changes, analyzed the whole picture, and consulted others. When introducing bell schedule changes or major master schedule changes, considering school culture and the readiness for a change of this magnitude is vital. A significant amount of time should be dedicated to determining the human impact through large- and small- group meetings with teachers, parents, and students. Schedule changes can be very complex so analyzing the whole picture is crucial. While the schedule may be what is in the foreground, other background issues will likely surface, many of which could fracture the faculty. Unless the schedule is inadvertently harming a group of students, a major scheduling change should not be pursued. Scheduling decisions should be made in consultation with the central office and all three problem-solving processes: Data, improvement, and stakeholder focus should be fully considered.

Summary

In this chapter, principals communicated about programmatic or policy changes that they introduced. In some cases, long-standing unethical practices were identified after a thorough examination of conclusive evidence. Close communication with the central office influenced how alleged faculty sexual misconduct cases were managed and how faculty mediation was initiated. Confidentiality and state laws were considered. Experienced knowledgeable principals, who had consulted their faculty, staff, and the central office, carefully introduced changes to the bell schedule. Recounting her decision to tackle minor changes in the schedule, Ms. Perez (MA) mentioned, "Difficult decisions have to do with not necessarily what's best for the school, but you have to make them because of lack of resources, so it's a decision that you may not necessarily want to happen." Principals also decided when and how to resist the central office mandates that were not beneficial to the school community.

Chapter 7 Case Study

Ms. Cantrell (MA) faced the daunting task of moving a school to another site amid fierce political pressure. It is wise to cautiously examine all options and to explore the political landscape. If it becomes apparent that the decision is a fait accompli, it may not be the battle to engage in. As you read the case study outlined here, if you were the school principal, how would you handle a mandatory school move?

CASE STUDY #6

Mandatory School Move

Ms. Cantrell (MA) was faced with an untenable decision. She was informed by the superintendent that her school was going to be required to move to a location in another part of the city and expand by 100 to 120 students. She was also told that they would need to accept the building as is with some upgrades to science labs. This move was part of a larger district plan to move seven schools to other locations. For Torbay Kent High School, the move came as a complete surprise. Principal Cantrell was not aware that decisions were being made to sell the building where her small school was located that shared space with another district high school. Initially Principal Cantrell needed to decide how she would convey the decision to her school community. Would she cooperate with the district and tell her staff and others that this move was what they had to do or would she resist the move? If she resisted the move, how would she resist? Ms. Cantrell was notified that the school department was going to issue a public statement. The school department developed written communication from each principal in each of the seven schools that perfidiously stated that the decision to move the schools had been collaborative. Ms. Cantrell was told by the superintendent to sign and distribute the letter to her families.

As Ms. Cantrell wrestled with whether or not to resist the move, she had meetings with a number of people in the district. She soon found out that the other school that Torbay Kent High School shared the building with was staying in the building and not being forced to move. Contrary to what she had been told, the building was not being sold after all. Ms. Cantrell also discovered that the mayor was supportive of the move. Ms. Cantrell had the added challenge of a small contingent of teachers who seemed determined to fight the move until the end. They were uninterested in considering renovations at the new building. They did not want to accept the fact that their school would have to move.

After several weeks of speeches before the school committee, the school department indicated that it would put $3 million into renovating the new building. The dollars allocated were insufficient. The school committee reconsidered, then passed a measure for $12 million, which the city council later cut to $10 million. Finally, the school committee was able to get the mayor to agree that they would not lose the elevator, science labs, and cafeteria that they had in their current building. That agreement meant that they had to build an addition to have a cafeteria. Ms. Cantrell had been offered a satellite kitchen rather than a full-service kitchen. She was mulling over whether she should resist the move given that 69% of her students qualify for free and reduced lunch, and she had heard other principals with satellite kitchens share that too much food is thrown away. Being faced with an obligatory school move, with very little input, can be a harrowing experience even for an experienced principal.

REFLECTIVE QUESTIONS

Develop a summary of what you know about what happened. What else would you like to know? You have several decisions to make:

1. What should Principal Cantrell communicate about the decision to her school community?

2. Should Ms. Cantrell cooperate with the district and tell her staff and others this move was what they had to do or should she resist the move?

3. If Ms. Cantrell resisted the move, how would she resist?

4. Should Ms. Cantrell sign and distribute the letter developed by the school department?

5. The superintendent wanted all schools to be notified at the same time. What issues might that present for Ms. Cantrell's school?

6. What are Ms. Cantrell's political alternatives given that she has been informed that her school is required to move?

7. Should Ms. Cantrell adhere to the stipulation that her school have a satellite kitchen rather than a full-size kitchen?

Turn to the Resources section in the back for a summary of how Ms. Cantrell handled this case.

8

Decisions That Improve African American and Latino Student Achievement

My decision was to remove the hurdles to Honors and AP courses, and I eliminated the arbitrary placement. As a direct result, there were more African American and Latino students in accelerated courses being more successful.

Dr. Manning, Principal—Massachusetts

Public school principals are leading increasingly diverse student populations. Fifteen years ago, Latinos surpassed Blacks as the country's largest minority (National Center for Education Statistics [NCES], 2007). In the United States, racial minority populations are growing, with Latinos representing most of the population growth. It is projected that in 2043, assuming lower than expected immigration rates, the United States will become a majority-minority nation (U.S. Census Bureau, 2012).

Whites currently represent 63% of the population, Latinos represent 17%, Blacks represent 12%, and Asians represent 5%. By 2050, Whites will decrease to 47% of the population. Latinos are projected to increase to 26% of the population, Blacks are expected to increase slightly to 13%, and Asians are expected to increase to 9% (McLaughlin, 2013; Taylor & Cohn, 2012)

From 2000 to 2010, the percentage of White students enrolled in public schools decreased from 61% to 52%, Latino public school enrollment increased from 16% to 23%, African American public school enrollment decreased from 17% to 16%, and Asian public school enrollment increased from 4% to 5% (Nachazel & Dzoiba, 2013). On several measures, including Advanced Placement (AP) scores, SAT scores, college graduation rates, and **NAEP** (National Assessment of Educational Progress, or the Nation's Report card), and math and reading scores, African American and Latino students have not been as successful as White students (College Board, 2013a, 2013b; McLaughlin, 2013; NCES, 2007, 2014).

Given the growth of minority populations and their lack of success in public schools, it is incumbent upon principals to address the performance of minorities and consider how decisions that are made affect minority student performance. This chapter includes the experiences of principals and their courageous decisions to introduce changes in structures, in the climate, and ultimately in the performance of their African American and Latino students.

Dr. Manning: Eliminating Course Access Barriers for Students of Color

Dr. Manning (MA) made the unprecedented decision to revamp the Honors and AP course enrollment process at her elite, traditional high school. At the time she made her decision, students were required to negotiate teachers' AP and Honors requirements. Some teachers required a test. Others required an information session or a paper. Dr. Manning stated that she felt very strongly that there were too many hurdles that prevented students, particularly African American and Latino students, from accessing courses. When the students had to negotiate with teachers, the students who were more savvy or had experience negotiating with teachers had an advantage. When Dr. Manning made the decision to remove the advantages, she incensed many of her parents and faculty. The parents of the high-performing students were unhappy about removing the eligibility requirements for taking Honors courses. Dr. Manning described faculty members who had been teaching AP courses as privileged members of the faculty. They had smaller class sizes and fewer classes. Many of the students in AP courses had been hand-selected by teachers. To address faculty concerns about the proposed changes, Dr. Manning created a working group of faculty and administrators who were charged with developing policy for AP and Honors courses. The faculty group determined that any student who had a C or higher in the preceding course would be eligible to take the AP course. At Dr. Manning's school, students are typically allowed to take a maximum of three AP courses at a time and can only take four AP courses with special permission. During the years of transitioning to a new policy, Dr. Manning communicated her prediction that AP scores might be slightly lower, but the priority was increased student participation.

As a result of the Honors and AP changes, more African American and Latino students enrolled in AP and Honors courses. After 4 years, even though they have increased their AP participation by 30%, the percentage of students scoring 3 or above has not decreased. Dr. Manning credits her faculty with that success.

Dr. Manning placed herself in a precarious position when she knowingly replaced traditions that unfairly advantaged her most entitled student population. There are significant political risks involved when a decision is made to dismantle privilege and counter a powerful group of parents and faculty. As she led the efforts to implement an audacious change, Dr. Manning examined multiple perspectives, investigated current practices, and met regularly with her faculty. She assessed the impact of the decision on her school's culture, her students, and her faculty and anticipated parental concerns. Dr. Manning was motivated by her core values of equity, excellence, and consistency. Dr. Manning was well aware that African American and Latino students were underrepresented in AP courses in her school.

Moreover, African Americans and Latinos have been underrepresented nationally in AP courses. Of the African American students in the graduating class of 2013, only 9.2% took an AP class. Only 18.8% of Latinos in the class of 2013 took an AP class. In contrast, 55.9% of White students in the class of 2013 took an AP class. Students earning a score of 3 or above on AP tests are eligible to earn college credit. According to the College Board (2013) *AP Report to the Nation* (see Table 8.1), only 4.6% of Blacks earned a passing score on an AP exam. Only 16.9% of Latinos earned a passing score. The percentage of White students that earned a passing score was 61.3%.

Table 8.1   AP Test Takers by Race—Class of 2013

Race	Percentage of the Graduating Class	Percentage of AP Test Takers	Percentage of Students Who Scored 3+ on AP Exams
Blacks	14.5	9.2	4.6
Latinos	18.8	18.8	16.9
Whites	58.3	55.9	61.3

Source: Data derived from *The 10th Annual AP® Report to the Nation* © 2013. The College Board. www.collegeboard.org. Reproduced with permission.

In spite of the potential repercussions, courageous principals address school policies and practices that perpetuate the achievement gap in their schools. Two other principals shared similar decisions that they had made to ensure that AP courses were open to all students. Ms. Perez (MA) stated that a number of shifts were made in the AP offerings at her exclusive urban high school. "We have made a lot of changes to AP courses to make them equally accessible to all students. Students used to have to take Economics before taking AP Economics. Now there are no prerequisites, but there are recommendations." If a student is doing well, faculty members strongly encourage the student to take Honors classes. Students can also sign up without a recommendation provided that they have a grade of B or higher. Some exceptions are entertained particularly if students indicate that they are willing to do the work. At Ms. Perez's school, extra steps are taken to consult with teachers and counselors before a student is denied access into an AP course.

> "I met with the guidance department, and when I saw that our top African American and Latino students were not in Honors and Advanced Placement courses, I asked why." Principal Adams (NC)

Mr. Adams (NC) described his school's intentional placement of African American students into advanced courses. "I met with the guidance department, and when I saw that our top African American and Latino students were not in Honors and Advanced Placement courses, I asked why." Mr. Adams made it clear to his counselors that he expected to see more African American and Latino students enrolled in advanced classes. Rather than ignore glaring disparities, principals who prioritized the performance of their minority students noticed the gaps and worked with faculty members to develop plans to make significant changes.

Dr. Zenga: Using Data to Narrow the Gap

Dr. Zenga (MA) made several decisions that have contributed to closing the gap at her affluent suburban high school. Though proudly touting her school's recent success, Dr. Zenga describes those decisions as controversial. Dr. Zenga was compelled to justify her focus on the gap to her faculty and to her highly involved parent community. Dr. Zenga asserted, "I feel very strongly that we have a very difficult time talking about issues of class that really affect my students. We have focused on issues of race and class, and teachers are working very hard with Black students, and we've seen a lot of increase in achievement."

A Focus on Student Data

Initially, Dr. Zenga made the decision to focus on data and to engage her faculty in data discussions about race, class, and achievement. Dr. Zenga described herself as a data geek and mentioned that when she became the principal at Cumbria Thurrock High School over 8 years ago, it had a 12% failure rate on the Massachusetts Comprehensive Assessment System (MCAS), which is used to assess 10th-grade students in English/Language Arts (ELA), Mathematics, and Science.

> ### Dr. Zenga's Decisions to Close the Achievement Gap
>
> 1. Focusing on student data and work with faculty on issues related to class, race, and achievement.
>
> 2. Developing an African American Scholars Program.

Dr. Zenga continued, "I use data a lot in making and communicating my decisions. You can't refute it. We focused on a school-wide goal of closing the gap." Dr. Zenga referenced the bell curve and explained her school's focus on what she dubbed the mountain. Typically used in statistics, the bell curve has a shape that is similar to a bell. The bell curve has a mean that is located in the center. The tails at either end of the bell represent the lowest and highest points in a data set. The bell curve is also described as a normal distribution with 50% of the numbers that are less than the mean and 50% of the numbers that are greater than the mean. Fendler and Muzaffar (2008) stated,

Table 8.2   MCAS Achievement Levels

MCAS Level	Level Descriptions
Advanced (A) Grades 3–8 and 10	Students demonstrate a comprehensive and in-depth understanding of rigorous subject matter and provide sophisticated solutions to complex problems.
Proficient (P) Grades 3–8 and 10	Students demonstrate a solid understanding of challenging subject matter and solve a wide variety of problems.
Needs Improvement (NI) Grades 3–8 and 10	Students demonstrate a partial understanding of subject matter and solve some simple problems.
Warning/Failing (W/F) W—Grades 3–8 F—Grade 10	Students demonstrate a minimal understanding of subject matter and do not solve simple problems.

Source: Massachusetts Department of Elementary and Secondary Education School District Profiles 2012 Complete Report Cards, 2013 Complete Report Cards.

Known popularly as the bell curve, and mathematically as the Gaussian curve, this model holds that most phenomena occur around a middle point, while few occur at either the high or low extreme ends. An assumption of bell-curve distribution permeates educational projects on several dimensions. . . . (p. 63)

Bell Curve

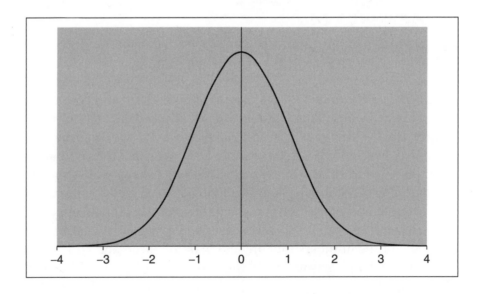

Dr. Zenga asserted, "We had no Black students fail the ELA MCAS. We had one low-income student out of five fail the Math. No Black students failed." For the past 2 years, Cumbria Thurrock High School has boasted a zero failure rate for African Americans and Latinos on the ELA MCAS.

We focused on the tail (the lowest achieving students) for the first 6 years, and now the majority of the kids are in the mountain so they are equally represented in the mountain. We've got to move the mountain. The next work is to see that Black and low-income students are proportionally represented in higher level courses (moving the mountain). Most (other) schools in America are trying to make sure that failure doesn't happen.

> "We had no Black students fail the ELA MCAS. We had one low-income student of five fail the Math. No Black students failed." Principal Zenga (MA)

As Dr. Zenga pointed out, "The data show that we have really narrowed the achievement gap for Black and low-income students." The gap for Latino students has also narrowed significantly. Dr. Zenga's description of the mountain refers to students who are in the mean, that is, average performers. To reiterate, *moving the mountain* refers to moving average performers into advanced (AP or Honors) classes. Dr. Zenga's leadership in closing the gap over the past 6 years has resulted in zero failures in ELA for Black and Latino students (Table 8.3). Although their

Table 8.3   Cumbria Thurrock High School

MCAS ELA 2013 and 2012—Grade 10				
	Advanced/Proficient		Fail	
Race	2013	2012	2013	2012
Whites	98%	99%	1%	0%
Blacks	93%	95%	0%	0%
Latinos	90%	90%	0%	0%

Source: Adapted from Massachusetts Department of Elementary and Secondary Education School District Profiles: 2012 Complete Report Cards, 2013 Complete Report Cards.

Balance of students earned Needs Improvement as a designation.

work to get to zero failures in Math will continue (Table 8.4), Dr. Zenga has now shifted the focus of her faculty to increasing the number of African Americans and Latinos in advanced courses.

Table 8.4   Cumbria Thurrock High School

MCAS Math 2013 and 2012—Grade 10				
	Advanced/Proficient		*Fail*	
Race	*2013*	*2012*	*2013*	*2012*
Whites	95%	96%	2%	2%
Blacks	73%	89%	7%	0%
Latinos	71%	86%	4%	0%

Source: Adapted from Massachusetts Department of Elementary and Secondary Education School District Profiles: 2012 Complete Report Cards, 2013 Complete Report Cards.

Balance of students earned Needs Improvement as a designation.

An African American Scholars Program

Another decision that Dr. Zenga made that contributed to closing the gap at her school was to support and develop an African American Scholars Program. Dr. Zenga claimed, "We are purposely supporting students to move into the higher courses. We created a Black Scholars Program based on the data. I can justify that. Black kids are not in the upper level classes at the same rate." Like Dr. Manning (MA), Dr. Zenga was motivated by her core values. As illustrated in Chapter 2, Dr. Zenga intentionally works with her faculty on matters that pertain to race, class, and academic achievement. One of Dr. Zenga's faculty members developed the idea of the Black Scholars Program and several faculty members participated in the program's development. To be eligible to be part of the program, students must earn a B– or higher class average and take at least one Honors or AP class. Students must also participate in Black history seminars, take a leadership course that is taught by English teachers, enroll in an internship, participate in an extracurricular activity, exhibit leadership, and complete service learning hours. Although initially developed for Black students, the program has expanded to also include Latino students. Students meet weekly during homeroom, and faculty advisors are selected for each scholar. Upon graduation, students are provided with scholarships.

Mr. Starnes: Balancing the Needs of Low-Achieving and Advanced Students

Principal Starnes (MA), who is a principal in the same district as Dr. Zenga, shared his sentiments about educating African American and Latino students in his building. "One of the things that we've identified is some stark achievement gaps. The data team established gaps between White and Latino students despite years of progressive antiracism." Mr. Starnes made a decision to prioritize closing the gap. Using similar language about the mountain (average performers) and the tail (lowest performers) as he discussed student performance, Mr. Starnes added, "We talked about eliminating the tail and moving the mountain. We consciously decided to work on eliminating the tail first." In data teams, faculty discussed how to significantly reduce and ultimately eliminate the number of students who were not performing at grade level.

> ### Mr. Starnes's Decisions to Close the Gap
>
> 1. Focusing resources and attention on the gap; providing leadership for a Data Team
> 2. Developing a school-wide focus on the tail (low-achieving minority students)
> 3. Establishing a timeline and a pilot that focuses on advanced students
> 4. Targeting instruction in lower level classes

Mr. Starnes also found the low numbers of minority students in AP courses to be disconcerting. After working at his high school for 5 years, Mr. Starnes initiated conversations with his faculty about moving the mountain, which is identifying average performers and encouraging students to enroll in advanced classes. Mr. Starnes questioned his faculty about the potential impediments. He appeared to be displeased about the resistance to focusing on moving the mountain and the tail simultaneously. Mr. Starnes continued, "Here's the dilemma: Do I trust them? That is, do I trust that they share my goal to move the mountain? These are the people who have to do the work."

> "I want us to be better at working with kids who struggle. . . . We have kids getting Cs in easier classes." Principal Starnes (MA)

Mr. Starnes had to decide what aspect of the gap to focus on—underperforming students or moving students into upper level classes. He also had to decide when to shift the school-wide focus. Mr. Starnes reluctantly acquiesced to his department chairs' insistence that the work on the tail had not yet reached a point where they were ready to turn their attention to the mountain. He validated the importance of listening to his faculty and added that is part of his job. Mr. Starnes expressed, "I want us to be better at working with kids who struggle, our D and F kids. We have kids getting Cs in easier classes." While acknowledging the limitations to what he could ask his faculty to focus on simultaneously, Mr. Starnes noted that it was a hard decision to back away from a school-wide focus on advanced students. Mr. Starnes consented to postponing school-wide efforts, adding that they will spend one more year focusing on students who are struggling. As the faculty improve their ability to work with struggling students, they will initiate strategic efforts geared toward work with advanced students.

Another decision Mr. Starnes made was to prioritize instruction. "The reality check for me was we need to really focus on the instructional level in our lower curriculum classes. It is new for teachers. I taught it, you didn't get it, maybe I should teach it in a different way." Mr. Starnes acknowledged the importance of monitoring lower level classes to ensure that quality instruction was taking place. Additionally, Mr. Starnes has been working to infuse new thinking into the culture of his school so that teachers concentrate on what the students have learned, not just what they have taught. Ball and Forzani (2011) advocate for high-leverage teaching strategies that focus on teaching practice that results in student learning: "The fundamental professional imperatives of teaching are to help students to master academic knowledge and skill, and to support their social and emotional development" (p. 19).

> "The reality check for me was we need to really focus on the instructional level in our lower curriculum classes. It is new for teachers. I taught it, you didn't get it, maybe I should teach it in a different way."
> Principal Starnes (MA)

Last, Mr. Starnes decided to begin some pilots with small groups of minority students who had the potential to be placed into advanced classes. Mr. Starnes described a program that had been implemented: "We are taking kids who are African American who otherwise wouldn't be taking an Advanced Placement course. We got three 5s, a 3, and a 1. We are creating a pathway to Calculus." Although he did not specify the total number of program participants, Mr. Starnes mentioned that five students had taken AP tests.

Four of the five students passed. As mentioned earlier in the chapter, students must earn a 3 out of a possible 5 on an AP test to receive a passing score. Given that a 5 is the highest attainable score, it is remarkable that three of the five students earned 5s. While five student test-takers is a small number, expanding the number of African American students taking AP Calculus is laudable.

Ms. Cantrell: Focusing on African American and Latino Males

Ms. Cantrell's (MA) decision to close the gap at her small urban high school has led to dramatic improvements. Ms. Cantrell led a 2-year professional development focus on African American males. Ms. Cantrell declared, "Our school has been commended and recognized by the U.S. Department of Education over the past few years, and our males of color have been recognized for higher achievement (better than state and national averages). Our Latino males have been recognized by the Gaston Institute as a school where Latino students excel." The Mauricio Gaston Institute for Latino Community Development and Public Policy at the University of Massachusetts, Boston, focuses on notifying public officials and the Latino community about policy matters that are crucial to Latinos. The Gaston Institute touted Torbay Kent's success with Latino students, namely the school's diversity, core values, habits of mind, and safety protocols. Torbay Kent's Latino and African American students have experienced increased achievement over time.

Ms. Cantrell's Decisions to Close the Gap

1. Leading a 2-year professional development focus on African American males

2. Supporting programs for Latino and African American males

3. Moving Torbay Kent High School toward a college preparatory focus

---

At Ms. Cantrell's school the 4-year graduation rate is 90% and the drop-out rate is 2%. Ninety-five percent of her students (40% Black and 47% Latino) go to 4-year colleges. Ms. Cantrell supported

African American male counselors at Torbay Kent High School in the development of a program for men of color that focuses on managing society's expectations and fulfilling dreams. Male students that participate in the program attend a retreat, weekly meetings, and are involved in leadership and service learning. A trip to Historically Black Colleges and Universities is also incorporated. Two other groups at Torbay Kent High School concentrate on male health and fitness and academic, social, and emotional growth for Latino and African American males.

Regarding state assessments, Torbay Kent Latino and African American students are performing above state averages. As illustrated in Table 8.5, Blacks and Latinos had a zero failure rate on the MCAS English/Language Arts in 2012 and 2013. For the Math MCAS, Blacks had a zero failure rate in 2012 and 2013 and Latinos had a zero failure rate in 2012 and 2.6% failure rate in 2013 (see Table 8.6). Ms. Cantrell added, "Our students are doing better, but there is a gap between Black and Latino students. A lot of the approaches to English Language Learners should be used in approaching African American students in teaching literacy." At Torbay Kent, literacy approaches include helping students develop academic vocabulary and strategies similar to those promoted by the Sheltered Instruction Observation Protocol (SIOP), which "emphasizes the importance of language development across the curriculum, as well as providing ample opportunity for students to

Table 8.5   Torbay Kent High School

MCAS ELA 2013 and 2012—Grade 10				
	Advanced/Proficient		*Fail*	
Race	*2013*	*2012*	*2013*	*2012*
Whites	(Fewer than 10 students—data not reported)			
Blacks	89.9%	85%	0%	0%
Latinos	97.3%	97%	0%	0%

Source: Adapted from Massachusetts Department of Elementary and Secondary Education School District Profiles: 2012 Complete Report Cards, 2013 Complete Report Cards.

Balance of students earned Needs Improvement as a designation.

practice reading, writing, speaking, and listening skills " (Echevarria, Richards-Tutor, Chinn, & Ratleff, 2011, p. 428).

Table 8.6   Torbay Kent High School

MCAS Math 2013 and 2012—Grade 10				
	Advanced/Proficient		Fail	
Race	2013	2012	2013	2012
Whites	(Fewer than 10 students—data not reported)			
Blacks	83.4%	69%	0%	0%
Latinos	79%	91%	2.6%	0%

Source: Adapted from Massachusetts Department of Elementary and Secondary Education School District Profiles: 2012 Complete Report Cards, 2013 Complete Report Cards.

Balance of students earned Needs Improvement as a designation.

Another decision Ms. Cantrell made that contributed to closing the gap was to lead a change to move Torbay Kent toward becoming a college preparatory high school. Ms. Cantrell mentioned, "It was more of a belief of preparing students for adulthood, to be good citizens. It never had a focus on college. I took the stance that getting a 4-year degree was necessary for preparing students for adulthood." Ms. Cantrell added that it was an easy decision, but several difficult conversations with faculty ensued. Moving toward being a college preparatory high school would require many changes in the courses offered and the way the school functioned.

Mr. Henry: Counseling First-Generation College Students

After decisions are made to support high minority student achievement, which result in a breadth of college alternatives for students, what type of counseling promotes the best options? Principal Henry (NC), a White male principal, recalled an experience with Sharon, one of his African American 12th graders. Sharon had a 4.5 GPA. Her mother, a single mom, works at Weiner Works (a local hot dog restaurant). "I told Sharon, you can go anywhere (to college) you want for free. Anywhere on Earth. Mom would not sign the FAFSA (Free Application for Federal Student Aid). She said, 'I told you 4,326 times. I'm not signing the paperwork.'"

Principal Henry recognized that with a 4.5 GPA, Sharon would be an excellent candidate for a highly selective university. He encouraged Sharon to apply to several colleges out of state, including a well-respected Historically Black College for Women, Spelman College. Sharon had applied to a small, noncompetitive private college. "I said, 'Honey we're not going there.' We applied to Winston Salem State, North Carolina Agricultural & Technical State University, and we got her down to Atlanta. Sharon got into Spelman College." On the subject of financial aid, Mr. Henry added that he had to convince Sharon's mother that a student loan was a plausible means of paying for college expenses. Principal Henry acknowledged Sharon's mother's concerns about having a bill for college expenses, but he informed her that it would be Sharon's bill when she graduated from college. He continued by describing the importance of catching his students who come from poor neighborhoods in time so that they had the option of attending college. At Mr. Henry's school, he added that they have great SAT scores and offer the most AP courses in the district so there are plenty of options for college-bound students.

High expectations for students of color need to be maintained throughout the college application process. Students who have been challenged to take advanced courses should be obliged to apply to highly selective colleges. The counseling process should be individualized and tailored toward working with first-generation students. When working with minority students, it should be understood that not all minority students need the same level of counseling. First-generation minority students do not have the same college counseling needs as those from an affluent or middle-class family whose parents are college educated.

Using Data to Analyze the Performance of African American and Latino Students

In addition to Dr. Zenga's decision to focus on data, other principals shared how their decisions to concentrate on data resulted in improved achievement for students of color. Principal Wallace (MD) divulged, "What we do weekly is look at pockets of data. We said this is what your scores look like on the state standard." Principal Wallace meets with her faculty on a weekly basis about student data then faculty members are expected to communicate with students about their individual performance on state standards. Principal Wallace explained, "Teachers are also generating their own student-based academic reports, and they are required to meet with students three times a trimester and identify the subscores or the indicators that the student is weak in and develop a plan." Principal Wallace has seen six times as many students passing the Maryland High School Assessment now than when she arrived 3 years ago.

> "What we do weekly is look at pockets of data. We said this is what your scores look like on the state standard." Principal Wallace (MD)

Ms. Lyons (NC) described the lenses through which she views her minority students. "I look at the data. I see them as students, future college students, citizens of the community. Our expectation is high achievement. I look at areas where students are not growing, and I make decisions." Her image of her students guides the decisions she makes about how to address their needs. Additionally Ms. Lyons considers areas of low growth and how the schedule augments or detracts from learning at her school. "When is the optimal learning time? Are students involved in sports? Can I move the schedule around so they can participate in sports in their district school so that they don't miss out on their core subjects? Ms. Lyons is the principal of an Early College High School. She is aware that the requirement for students to travel to their district high school to participate in sports contributes to her low male student enrollment. Ms. Lyons also added, "I'm constantly comparing our data to the other schools by ethnicity." Ms. Lyons is knowledgeable about the performance of her minority students, and she is conscious about whether her students are matching or exceeding the performance

> "I look at areas where students are not growing, and I make decisions." Principal Lyons (NC)

of other minority students in her district. Ms. Lyons utilizes these data to make decisions to improve student learning.

Mr. Adams (NC) also added, "Data. That is what drives the decisions we make, using EOC data, **EVAAS** data, discipline data, VOCATs. I have a half-day (training for staff) focused on data. How many kids were suspended? What is their race?" Mr. Adams made the decision to regularly review data and pay particular attention to the academic and disciplinary performance of his African American and Latino students particularly using End of Course (EOC), VOCATs standardized test data, and EVAAS growth scores. At Mr. Peppers's school in North Carolina, African American students are the majority. Mr. Peppers mentioned, "Student achievement. We look at test scores. We look at which teachers have the most discipline referrals and what are the instances? Student achievement and discipline actions make up a lot of decisions." Many of Mr. Peppers's decisions include deciphering achievement and discipline data. He is constantly asking what the data tell him about the areas in which students are not performing well. He also utilizes the data to facilitate conversations about student behavioral responses. Mr. Peppers identifies patterns and draws conclusions that assist him with improving the performance of his African American students.

In addition to decisions about data, several principals in Massachusetts, North Carolina, and Maryland elaborated on the decisions that they made to increase the performance of their African American and Latino students.

Decisions Made to Improve Minority Student Achievement

1. Deciding to hire diverse, excellent teachers
2. Providing quality instruction and wraparound services

Hiring Diverse, Excellent Teachers

Principal Rodriguez (MA) highlighted her decision to concentrate on hiring the best teachers for her school that consists of a majority of Latino students. Principal Rodriguez hires teachers who are capable of working with a highly diverse population of students, many of whom are newcomers to this country, have below-grade-level skills in literacy, or who may have had interrupted learning. In Chapter 6, principals described their decisions to hire caring, competent teachers who developed positive, mutually respectful relationships with students. In addition to generally searching for the best teachers, Dr. Manning (MA) actively seeks out the best teachers of color. Dr. Manning has implemented a process whereby she targets the recruitment of minority teachers. Principals can increase the numbers of minority teacher applicants by recruiting at churches, sororities, fraternities, Historically Colleges and Universities (HBCUs), and Hispanic Serving Institutions (HSIs).

Ms. Lyons (NC) asserted, "I look at staff and get the diversity there for that (student) population. Getting to know the whole child, not letting any child fall between the cracks, and having that relationship not only with the student, but with the parent or guardian." Ms. Lyons has also decided to actively recruit a diverse faculty, and she provides leadership to teachers so that relationship building with students and families is an articulated priority. Ms. Lyons's school is an Early College High School based at a university in her district so her students are also exposed to the opportunities at the university. Ms. Lyons added, "You constantly have to encourage students that they have the ability." Perry, Steele, and Hilliard (2003) posit that there are "extra social, emotional, cognitive, and political competencies required of African American youth" in order for students to be academically successful (p. 4). Ms. Lyons recognized the importance of making sure that her minority students receive regular messages from teachers and administrators that they are capable of high academic achievement. Ms. Lyons promoted these strategies to improve achievement at her school.

Ms. Major (NC), the principal of another Early College High School in the same district, explained, "The Early College Program is one that targets underrepresented students in colleges and universities." Ms. Major specified, "We have to be culturally sensitive. Our teaching staff has fewer minorities. My teachers are awesome. They build relationships with the kids. The kids know that they are cared about regardless of what the teachers look like." In Chapter 3, several principals attested to the connection between their decisions to focus on student relationships and the development of a positive school culture. As a principal with a large minority population and a predominantly White faculty, Ms. Major communicated to her staff about the importance of **culturally responsive** instructional practices. Expert principals sought culturally responsive teachers capable of working with a highly diverse student population who prioritize student relationship building and propel students to attain high academic achievement.

Prioritizing Quality Instruction and Wraparound Services

Principal Jeffreys (MD) recounted her decisions aimed at closing the gap at her high-poverty, majority-minority urban school. Her emphasis is on quality instruction and providing wraparound services,

"Giving students multiple opportunities to meet with success. We had things like credit recovery before the district required it. We're here on Saturday. We put in place built-in interventions during the school day." Dr. Jeffreys indicated that at her school, she has a family community liaison and a full-time social worker. Although she is only budgeted to have a part-time social worker, Dr. Jeffreys requested a full-time social worker and was able to augment services by partnering with the University of Maryland to provide student interns. Dr. Jeffreys describes the social services support provided to students as wraparound services. "We participate in the youth works program—summer employment. Now the district encourages schools to be a site where they hire students. We are a career and technology education school." Students are required to complete internships and summer work hours, and Dr. Jeffreys works with community and business partnerships to make sure that her students are working at paying jobs. Boykin and Noguera (2011) propose a strategy that urban and rural high-poverty schools can utilize to build their capacity to support students and close the gap. Like the Comer Schools and Harlem Children's Schools full-service models, schools are advised to combine a "social service strategy with a well-thought out academic enrichment strategy" (p. 178).

Summary: Factors Considered in Decisions to Close the Achievement Gap

Principals who led changes in the performance of their African American and Latino students were driven by core values about equity and excellence. They recognized that increasing the achievement of a traditionally underperforming group of students would mean making adjustments to current school practices or policies that allowed the underachievement to be perpetuated. In some cases, the changes introduced infuriated entitled parents and students and also ostracized faculty members. It is vital to have a supportive central office, particularly when introducing controversial changes. Principals were willing to experience temporary discomfort to lead their faculty and school community in a direction that would ultimately be in the best interest of all students. The changes were not made insensitively—time was reserved for addressing the concerns raised by nonsupportive faculty members and meetings were held with concerned parents. Principals explained their rationale to their faculty and parent community to ensure families that their children's education would not be negatively impacted as a result of changes created to improve the achievement of minority students.

Principals who worked assiduously to close the gap at their schools invested time and resources in this effort. Moreover, closing the gap garnered school-wide attention. Principals also led intensive multiyear professional development that centered on African American males and empowered faculty and staff to create initiatives aimed at supporting the high academic achievement of minority students. High expectations for minority students were maintained throughout the college counseling process. Data were reviewed to determine optimal learning schedules to expose academic weaknesses and to identify vexing patterns. Discussions about data in weekly faculty conversations illuminated connections between standards and student performance and highlighted the importance of hiring and wraparound services. As has been illustrated, several principals in Massachusetts, Maryland, and North Carolina made pivotal decisions that resulted in closing the achievement gap in their schools.

Concluding Thoughts

This book attempts to elucidate for new or aspiring principals the most crucial aspects of difficult or complex decisions. Several factors were introduced that expert principals consider in decision making: the impact of the principal's core values on decision making, how a school's culture affects decision making, examining the scope of a difficult decision, and involving faculty and mentors in decision making. Principals asserted that it was important to thoroughly investigate and make sure that they had the documentation to support their decisions. Principals also discussed how they made policy decisions that affected students, difficult decisions about budgeting and staff, programmatic decisions and decisions that improved the academic performance of African American and Latino students. To make decisions that resulted in the improved performance of African American and Latino students, principals utilized strategies detailed in the first section of this book, namely, they were guided by their core values and consciously operated in conjunction with or strategically in opposition to their school's culture. Furthermore, principals examined the big picture, extended their field of attention, visualized a probable solution, considered how others would be impacted, and involved others in their decision making.

Insights: How Expert Principals Make Difficult Decisions

Part I: Factors Expert Principals Consider in Decision Making

1. **Key Problem-Solving Processes of Expert Principals**—Expert principals gathered data, analyzed scenarios, recounted relevant anecdotes, identified and overcame constraints, planned their approach, faced conflict, assessed the long-term outlook, stressed follow-up, focused on student program quality, delegated, and kept parents informed.

2. **Leadership Core Values**—Principals made decisions connected to the school mission, grounded decisions in law, remained steady and calm when making decisions, invested sufficient time in decision making, were willing to make controversial decisions, were transparent in their decision making, and allowed morality and ethics to guide decision making.

3. **School Culture**—Principals spent time getting to know the school culture and built trusting relationships before infusing change in the culture.

4. **Big Picture, Expanded Field of Attention, and Visualized Solutions**—When faced with a difficult decision, principals examined the whole picture, expanded their field of attention, visualized solutions through reflecting, considered how faculty and staff would be impacted, and determined if the decision was complex or difficult before deciding whether to include staff in the decision-making process. Principals also consulted mentors.

Part II: Making Difficult Decisions

5. **Decisions That Impact Students**—Principals questioned whether their decisions were in their students' best interest and thoughtfully made decisions that impacted students, including managing crises, making policy decisions based on student choices, implementing attendance changes to improve student work ethic and responsibility, and making recommendations about long-term suspensions or expulsions.

6. **Faculty and Staff**—Principals established trusting, caring school communities and invested a significant amount of time hiring

quality staff. It was in this type of environment that they willingly made difficult decisions about budgets and firing teachers, administrators, or coaches after conducting intense evaluations, collaborating with others in the evaluation process, and prioritizing nontenured teachers.

7. **Practices, Policies, and Programs**—Principals made audacious decisions to stop duplicitous faculty practices, the distribution of fraudulent transcripts, and the unauthorized use of the school building and investigated allegations of sexual misconduct. Principals also tackled changes in the master schedule and weighed the impact that central office would have on their decision making.

8. **Decisions That Improve African American and Latino Achievement**—When making decisions to improve the performance of African American and Latino students, principals eliminated obstacles that prevented African American and Latino students from enrolling in Honors and AP classes. Principals were guided by core values that propelled them even in the face of parental and faculty opposition. Closing the gap was attained through a series of school-wide goals and multiyear efforts. Additionally, principals hired culturally responsive teachers, provided wraparound services for students as needed, and utilized data to uncover deep-seated issues and to spearhead reform.

A Massachusetts principal, Ms. Langely, eloquently described the process of engaging in contemplative decision making when faced with a difficult or complex problem. Her approach exemplifies strategies for effective decision making.

> In general in my years in administration, the two places I go all the time in the decision making: What is the problem we are trying to solve? What evidence do we have? Before speaking to people, I'm thinking about the options and the unintended consequences and being very careful that I have the different perspectives and that I've given enough face time to the people who need to be heard, being very clear with the people about whether they have a say in the decision.

References

Ball, D. L., & Forzani, F. M. (2011). Building a common core for learning to teach and connecting professional learning to practice. *American Educator, 35*(2), 17–21, 38–39.

Boykin, A. W., & Noguera, P. (2011). *Creating the opportunity to learn: Moving from research to practice to close the achievement gap.* Alexandria, VA: ASCD.

Brenninkmeyer, L. D., & Spillane, J. P. (2008). Problem-solving processes of expert and typical school principals: A quantitative look. *School Leadership & Management, 28*(5), 435–468.

Brown, M. (2014, May 19). Update: State judge rules in favor of teachers group on tenure law. *News & Record.* Retrieved from http://www.news-record.com/news/article_543d7e02-dcea-11e3-8c38-001a4bcf6878.html

Bullock, K., James, C., & Jamieson, I. (1995). An exploratory study of novices and experts in educational management. *Educational Management and Administration, 23*(3), 197–205.

Chi, M. T. H., Glaser, R., & Farr, M. J. (1988). *The nature of expertise.* Hillsdale, NJ: Lawrence Erlbaum.

Cohen, J., Pickeral, T., & McCloskey, M. (2008/2009). The challenge of assessing school Climate. *Educational Leadership, 66*(4). Retrieved from http://www.ascd.org/publications/educational-leadership/dec08/vol66/num04/The-Challenge-of-Assessing-School-Climate.aspx

College Board. (2013a). *The 10th annual AP report to the nation.* Retrieved from http://apreport.collegeboard.org/

College Board. (2013b). *College-bound seniors total group profile report.* Retrieved from http://media.collegeboard.com/digitalServices/pdf/research/2013/TotalGroup-2013.pdf

Connolly, M., James, C., & Beales, B. (2011). Contrasting perspectives on organizational culture change in schools. *Journal of Educational Change, 12*(4), 421–439.

Copland, M. A. (2003). Developing prospective principals' problem-framing skills. *Journal of School Leadership, 13*(5), 529–548.

Davis, S. (2004). The myth of the rational decision maker: A framework for applying and enhancing heuristic and intuitive decision making by school leaders. *Journal of School Leadership, 14*(6), 621–652.

Dufour, R. (2007). In praise of top-down leadership. *School Administrator, 64*(10), 38–42.

Dufresne, P., & McKenzie, A. S. (2009). A culture of ethical leadership. *Principal Leadership, 10*(2), 36–39.

Echevarria, J., Richards-Tutor C., Chinn, V. P., & Ratleff, P. (2011). Did they get it? The role of fidelity in teaching English learners. *Journal of Adolescent & Adult Literacy, 54*(6), 425–434.

English, F. W. (2006). *Encyclopedia of educational leadership and administration.* Thousand Oaks, CA: Sage.

Fendler, L., & Muzaffar, I. (2008). The history of the bell curve: Sorting and the idea of normal. *Educational Theory, 58*(1), 63–82.

Fullan, M. (2008). *The six secrets of change: What the best leaders do to help their organizations survive and thrive.* San Francisco, CA: Jossey-Bass.

Fullan, M. (2011). *Change leader: Learning to do what matters most.* San Francisco, CA: Jossey-Bass.

Homer-Dixon, T. (2000, November 24). Leadership captive. *Toronto Globe and Mail,* p. A15.

Leithwood, K. A. (1995). Cognitive perspectives on school leadership. *Journal of School Leadership, 5*(2), 115–135.

Leithwood, K. A., & Stager, M. (1989). Expertise in principals' problem-solving. *Educational Administration Quarterly, 25*(2), 126–161.

Massachusetts G.L.c. 71, 37H.

Mattocks, T. C. (2006). Leadership and the law. In E. E. Davis (Ed.), *Qualities for effective leadership* (pp. 105–119). Lanham, MD: Rowan & Littlefield Education.

McLaughlin, D. V. (2012). The cultural symphony in schools: Effectively teaching African American and Latino high school students. *Teacher Education Journal of South Carolina, 12*(1), 113–120.

McLaughlin, D. V. (2013). Inside our world: How administrators can improve schools by learning from the experiences of African American and Latino high school students. *NCPEA Education Leadership Special Issue, 14*(2), 28–40.

Myers, N. J. (2008). Block scheduling that gets results. *Principal, 88*(2), 20–23.

Nachazel, T., & Dzoiba, A. (2013). *The condition of education 2013.* (NCES 2013-037). Washington, DC: National Center for Education Statistics, Institute of Education Sciences, U.S. Department of Education.

National Center for Education Statistics. (2007). *Status and trends in the education of racial and ethnic minorities* (NCES 2007-039). Washington, DC: Institute of Education Sciences, U.S. Department of Education.

National Center for Education Statistics. (2014). *The nation's report card. 2013 mathematics and reading grade 12 assessments* (NCES 2014-087). Washington, DC: Institute of Education Sciences, U.S. Department of Education.

National School Climate Council. (2007). *The school climate challenge: Narrowing the gap between school climate research and school climate policy, practice guidelines and teacher education policy.* New York, NY: Center for Social and Emotional Education; & Denver, CO: National Center for Learning and Citizenship, Education Commission of the States. Retrieved from http://csee.net/climate/aboutcsee/school_climate_challenge.pdf

Pauken, P. (2012). Are you prepared to defend the decisions you've made? Reflective equilibrium, situational appreciation, and the legal and moral decisions of school leaders. *Journal of School Leadership, 22*(2), 350–384.

Perry. T., Steele, C., & Hilliard, A. (2003). *Young, gifted and black: Promoting high achievement among African-American students.* Boston, MA: Beacon Press.

Shakeshaft, C. (2013). Know the warning signs of educator sexual misconduct. *Phi Delta Kappan, 94*(5), 8–13.

Spillane, J. P., & Healey, K. (2010). Conceptualizing school leadership and management from a distributed perspective. *Elementary Journal, 111*(2), 253–281.

Taylor, P., & Cohn, D. (2012). *A milestone en route to a majority minority nation.* Washington, DC: Pew Research Social & Demographic Trends.

U.S. Census Bureau. (2012). *U.S. Census Bureau projections show a slower growing, older, more diverse nation a half century from now.* Retrieved from https://www.census.gov/newsroom/releases/archives/population/cb12-243.html

U.S. Department of Health and Human Services, Child Welfare Information Gateway. (2012). *Mandatory reporters of child abuse and neglect.* Retrieved from https://www.childwelfare.gov/systemwide/laws_policies/statutes/manda.pdf

Winerip, M. (2013, March 29). Ex-schools chief in Atlanta is indicted in testing scandal. *New York Times.* Retrieved from http://www.nytimes.com/2013/03/30/us/former-school-chief-in-atlanta-indicted-in-cheating-scandal.html?pagewanted=all&_r=1&

Zelkowski, J. (2010). Secondary mathematics: Four credits, block schedules, continuous enrollment? What maximizes college readiness? *Mathematics Educator, 20*(1), 8–21.

Resources

Classroom Walkthrough Form

School: _____ Teacher: _____ Date: _____

Class: _____ Observer: _____ Time: _____

LessonPlans: _____ Time on Task/Lesson Focus: _____

__ Yes __ No Lesson plans are available   __ Yes __ No Students understand lesson focus

__ Yes __ No Objectives align with pacing guides   __ Yes __ No Class started quickly

Content Knowledge	Facilitating Learning	Classroom Management	Establishes Respectful Learning Environment for Diverse Learners
__ Understands content, makes it meaningful to students __ Utilizes effective questioning strategies __ Uses key vocabulary and concepts __ Differentiates Instruction	__ Links to prior learning __ Plans instruction appropriately __ Utilizes a variety of instructional strategies __ Integrates technology __ Makes real-world connections with content __ Provides rigorous instruction	__ Monitors behavior __ Stops inappropriate behavior __ Routines are established __ Transitions are smooth __ Students are engaged	__ Utilizes culturally proficient instructional examples, perspectives, and experiences __ Culturally diverse learners participate in classroom activities __ Creates positive, mutually respectful classroom climate __ Adjusts teaching for the students with special needs

Strengths:		Areas for Improvement:	

Copy for teacher. Copy for Administrator.

Current Bell Schedule

Regular Release	Early Release	X Block	Day 1	Day 2	Day 3	Day 4	Day 5	Day 6	Day 7	Day 8
7:25 → 7:30	7:25 → 7:30	7:25 → 7:30	HR	HR	HR	HR	HR	HR	HR	HR
7:34 → 8:21	7:34 → 8:08	7:34 → 8:10	A	H	G	F	E	D	C	B
8:25 → 9:12	8:12 → 8:45	8:14 → 8:51	B	A	H	G	F	E	D	C
9:16 → 10:03	8:49 → 9:23	8:55 → 9:32	C	B	A	H	G	F	E	D
10:07 → 10:54	9:27 → 10:00	9:36 → 10:13	D	C	B	A	H	G	F	E
		10:17 → 10:54								

(Continued)

(Continued)

Regular Release	Early Release	X Block	Day 1	Day 2	Day 3	Day 4	Day 5	Day 6	Day 7	Day 8
10:54 → 12:19 LUNCH	10:04 → 10:38	10:54 → 12:19 LUNCH	E	D	C	B	A	H	G	F
12:23 → 1:10	10:42 → 11:15	12:23 → 1:10	F	E	D	C	B	A	H	G
1:14 → 2:02	11:15 → 12:42 LUNCH	1:14 → 2:02	G	F	E	D	C	B	A	H
Drop Block			H	G	F	E	D	C	B	A

REGULAR SCHEDULE AND X BLOCK LUNCH

1st Lunch
Lunch: 10:54–11:24
Class: 11:28–12:19

2nd Lunch (split class)
Class: 10:58–11:22
Lunch: 11:22–11:52
Class: 11:52–12:19

3rd Lunch
Class: 10:58–11:49
Lunch: 11:49–12:19

EARLY RELEASE WEDNESDAYS' LUNCH

1st Lunch
Lunch: 11:15–11:45
Class: 11:49–12:40

2nd Lunch (split class)
Class: 11:19–11:43
Lunch: 11:43–12:13
Class: 12:13–12:42

3rd Lunch
Class: 11:19–12:10
Lunch: 12:10–12:42

Proposed Bell Schedule

6×8 Schedule

8 Total Blocks/6-Period Day (six 57-minute periods, one 60-minute period)

Regular	*1*	*2*	*3*	*4*	*5*	*6*	*7*	*8*
HR 7:25–7:30 5″								
7:34–8:31 57″	A	B	C	D	A	B	C	D
8:35–9:32 57″	B	C	D	A	B	C	D	A
9:36–10:33 57″	C	D	A	B	C	D	A	B
10:33–12:03 60″ (Lunch)	E	F	G	H	E	F	G	H
12:04–1:01 57″	F	G	H	E	F	G	H	E
1:05–2:02 57″	G	H	E	F	G	H	E	F
Drop	**DH**	**AE**	**BF**	**CG**	**DH**	**AE**	**BF**	**CG**

Changes from present schedule:

Increase in length of blocks by 10 minutes

Morning rotation (A, B, C, D) and afternoon rotation (E, F, G, H)

Two blocks drop per day

Lunch Schedule

Lunch (30 minutes)	Class (60 minutes)
1st 10:33–11.03	11:03–12:03
2nd 11:03–11:33	10:33–11:03, 11:33–12:03
3rd 11:33–12:03	10:33–11:33

Principal Interview Questions

Name: Gender: School Name:

Introductory statement:

Thank you for your willingness to be in my study and do this interview with me today.

This study will investigate the decision-making practices of 21 high school principals in three states: Maryland, Massachusetts, and North Carolina. Your comments will be treated as strictly confidential; no names will ever be linked directly to your comments, so no one else will know what you said. Please feel free to say as much or as little as you like in response to my questions. There is no right answer—I just want to know what you think. During this interview, I will be taking notes using a notepad, or if permissible, I would like to use a laptop computer. If you would prefer I not use a laptop, I can simply use written notes. What is your preference?

1. How many years have you been a principal?

2. How many years have you been a principal at this high school?

3. How many years of experience did you have teaching before you became a principal?

4. How many years of experience did you have as an assistant principal, counselor, or district coordinator?

5. Where did you attend college, and what degrees did you earn?

6. What do you consider to be your race or ethnicity?

7. What were two of the most difficult or complex decisions that you have made, and what factors did you consider as you made the decisions?

   Decision #1:

   Decision #2:

8. What goes through your mind when you make decisions?

9. Did you have any help in making these decisions?

10. In general, how much time do you have to make decisions?

    a. Can you give me an example?

11. In general, what makes decisions difficult?

12. Can you talk about a decision that was especially difficult?

    a. What was your rationale for making this decision?
    b. What was the impact of the decision?

13. What, if anything, influenced how you made this decision?

14. Did prior knowledge or experience play a part?

    a. If so, can you talk about how?

15. Were you influenced by a philosophy or leadership style?

16. What else do you consider when making decisions?

    a. Do you have specific guiding principles?

       i. If so, can you tell me more about these?

17. What was the role of external influences on your decision making?

18. What's one of the easiest decisions you have made?

    a. What made it easy?

19. How would you describe the culture of your school? How, if at all, does the school's culture affect your decision making?

20. Briefly tell me about the performance of the African American and Latino students in your school.

21. What decisions, if any, have you made related to the performance of African American and Latino students in your school?

22. Do you use data in your decision making as you work on these issues? If so, how?

23. Would you describe your decision making as "analytical"?

    a. Can you say more about this?

24. Do you organize information categorically by chunking patterns of information into easily managed pieces?

    a. Can you say more about this?

25. Do you develop typical responses to thematically similar problem situations?

    a. Can you tell me more about this?

26. Can we briefly review some principal problem-solving processes? Which of these would you say you use regularly when making decisions? (A check mark or asterisk will be placed next to the ones identified.)

    Recounts relevant anecdotes

    Identifies, overcomes constraints

    Faces conflicts

    Focuses on student program quality

    Gathers data

    Keeps parents informed

    Delegates

    Plans approach

    Has long-term outlook

    Stresses follow-up

    Analyzes the scenario

    a. Would you like to say more about any of these processes?

27. To what extent do you visualize a solution to a dilemma?

    a. Do you anticipate the end result?

28. Do you ever use unconventional thinking? By unconventional, I am referring to thinking that could be termed unorthodox.

29. Do you ever use metaphorical thinking? This refers to the development of symbolic and visually descriptive pictures.

30. Do you use problem framing? That is, do you examine conceivable perspectives such as Bolman and Deal's (1) structural, (2) Human Resources, (3) political, and (4) symbolic frames?

Just a synopsis in case you are unfamiliar with these frames: Structural emphasizes rationality, structures, and rules. Human resource focuses on people, relationships, and empowerment.

Political focuses on competing interests, conflict, and negotiation. Symbolic emphasizes culture, rituals, and inspiration.

31. Do you center your mind through focused relaxation?

   a. Centering your mind refers to devoting significant amounts of time to meditation, concentrated thinking, and sufficient nighttime sleep. So restated, do you prioritize the importance of remaining mentally sharp?

32. How do you think your varied life experiences help you make decisions? Do you seek out these life experiences?

Resources

Chapter 1

Resolution: Case Study #1: It All Started So Well—How Poorly Made Decisions Can Sabotage a Principalship: Dr. Iona

1. Dr. Iona should have conducted a thorough investigation of the scheduling needs of her school, met with her Leadership Team about the proposed changes, and carefully considered the repercussions of a schedule change. Dr. Iona could also have consulted her area superintendent about her plans and solicited input.

Though she engaged in some meetings with teachers, Dr. Iona did not anticipate the problems that would arise with the new schedule. Potential pitfalls such as extraordinarily long lines in the cafeteria, teacher fatigue, and the impact of eating lunch at 10:40 a.m. should not have been dismissed. If Dr. Iona was unable to adequately address these concerns before the new schedule was introduced, the changes should not have been implemented. A scheduling change is a major undertaking that should not be introduced without a thoroughly developed implementation plan.

2. Dr. Iona should have created a process to obtain feedback about the new schedule change. If she had done this, teachers may not have felt the need to communicate their concerns to parents. Because Dr. Iona was so invested in the change, she missed overt signs that support for the schedule was waning. She should have discussed the changes with teachers during passing periods, in the cafeteria, and during scheduled input sessions. Dr. Iona might have learned about teacher concerns during these formal and informal conversations. While it is important not to vacillate once a decision has been made, room needs to made for input and adjustments if needed.

3. Ideally class changes are made before students and parents see the schedules. If changes need to be made after students have already been attending classes for 3 or more weeks, teachers, parents, students, and counselors should be part of the decision-making process. Classes should be balanced based on race, gender, and academic ability. Attention should be paid to the needs of English Language Learners and special education individualized education programs (IEPs) when making class changes. The needs of graduating seniors

and athletes should be considered where possible. Even in cases where students may not be especially fond of their teacher, after 3 weeks, routines have been established, friendships with classmates created, and teacher expectations communicated. Moving to a classroom with a new teacher represents the unknown and will be perceived by most as unpopular. The new class will likely have few volunteers and be smaller than the other classes since many parents and students will opt to stay where they are (even if the class is larger and overcrowded). The rules for the moves should be clearly articulated and consistently applied.

4. Dr. Iona failed to recognize that she was implementing too many changes too quickly. Teachers were not able to adjust to the first change before another change was introduced. While it is risky not to comply with central office mandates, principals should be willing to communicate with central office leaders at times when initiatives are ill timed or overwhelming for their staff. In cases where there are state mandates no such flexibility exists, but sometimes principals can make a plea for more time or a graduated rollout period for a new initiative. In this case, ultimately the pressure did not work. There was dissent so progress was stalled. Energy was diverted to focusing on fixing the environment rather than on improving student learning outcomes.

Chapter 1

Resolution: Case Study #2: Effectively Addressing an Egregious Error: Ms. Steadman

Using student initials, Ms. Steadman presented data to her counselors from 12 student transcripts that illustrated the transcript errors. Ms. Steadman communicated that what mattered was correcting the errors and developing a process to ensure that these types of errors did not reoccur.

1. In an effort to provide counselors with time to correct the errors, Ms. Steadman allowed them to spend faculty meeting time initially set aside for school-wide equity training to correct transcripts. Since the errors that had been discovered pertained to transcripts of African American and Latino students, counselors were told to primarily focus their attention on reviewing the transcripts of African American and Latino students in their part of the alphabet. As time allowed, their charge was to review the transcripts of all their other fragile learners and eventually to ensure that all transcripts were free of errors.

2. Ms. Steadman elected to focus on exposing the errors and reaching a solution so that these types of errors would not occur again. Ms. Steadman did not assign consequences to counselors who were responsible for the errors; instead she provided additional time for them to correct the errors.

3. Counselors were advised to communicate with parents and students about the errors on student transcripts.

Chapter 5

Resolution: Case Study #3: Distorted Yearbook Picture

1. Since Morant Surrey is such a large high school—about 1,900 students—and the yearbooks had already been printed and distributed to seniors, it was not possible to collect the books. It was also not financially feasible nor was there sufficient time before the end of the school year to reprint 1,900 yearbooks.

2. A thorough investigation took place before any consequences were assigned. Several students were interviewed and written statements were retrieved. Ms. Mobay, the yearbook teacher, was mortified. She had proofed the yearbook, but had not seen any of the distortions before the final printing. After the witness statements were gathered, Principal Steadman communicated with Mandy.

3. Due to the sensitive nature of this situation, parents were not contacted until after Principal Steadman was able to deduce what happened and after she had a written statement from Mandy.

4. Once Mandy admitted to the offense, Principal Steadman considered when she could issue a suspension. There were very few days left before final exams began and the last day of school for seniors was approaching quickly.

5. While it was tempting to consider taking away the prom or graduation, the prom had already taken place since it was so late in the year. Principal Steadman realized that graduation is usually more valued by parents and family members than students. Taking away graduation is an irrevocable decision that should only be considered under very dire circumstances when no other alternatives are available. Principal Steadman did not create any stipulations about not attending graduation as part of the consequences issued.

6. Mandy was also a member of the National Honor Society, but since the faculty committee is primarily responsible for making determinations about revoking membership, Principal Steadman provided the faculty advisor with the information about the offense. The faculty committee ultimately decided to remove Mandy from the National Honor Society.

7. Mandy had already been accepted to college so Mandy's father made the proactive decision to contact the university to inform them of the situation before the school was compelled to do so.

8. Principal Steadman had to contend with the media, though most communication was directed to central office. Helen's father decided to contact the local television station to share his daughter's story.

9. Regarding Mandy's consequences, she served a multiday suspension and she was required to pay to have a small number of yearbooks (10) reprinted so that Helen and her family could have a yearbook without the distortions, some copies could be printed and kept at the school, and Helen's friends who were featured on the same page could also receive pictures that were free from tampering.

10. Principal Steadman spent an inordinate amount of time meeting with families, students, teachers, and her school community. It was particularly important to spend time with Helen and provide her with guidance counselor support to help her cope with this difficult situation.

Chapter 5

Resolution: Case Study #4: Cyberbullying

1. Dr. Howell communicated with her assistant principal, Ms. Gray, and Martin's counselor to review any records or e-mail communication they had received from the Jaspers about Martin. Once it was determined that Ms. Gray had not been made aware of the bullying from the previous year, that was communicated to the Jaspers. Mrs. Jasper had communicated with the counselor but stated at that time that she did not want to pursue any action against Sam or Dianne. The counselor was encouraged to share this type of information with an assistant principal if provided by a parent in any future communication.

2. The Jaspers were exasperated so they were considering legal action. Dr. Howell provided them with the School Resource Officer's contact information so that they could talk with him about the process for filing charges against Sam and Dianne.

3. Dr. Howell communicated with the principal at Surrey Glen High School, Martin's current school, about providing support for Martin given the continuation of this harassment and his mental health needs.

4. Dr. Howell clarified the limitations of the school's jurisdiction. Consequences could only be assigned for Facebook threats that were issued at school or if the threats caused a substantial disruption to the school community. Dr. Howell encouraged the Jaspers to contact the local police about the incident that took place at the mall.

5. Suspensions were issued for Sam and Dianne for harassment and bullying.

Chapter 6

Resolution: Case Study #5:
Teacher Disregards District Policies

1. For the first incident, Dr. Zenga was compelled to assign disciplinary consequences. She suspended the student.

2. Following the first incident, Dr. Zenga had a meeting with Mr. Owen and gave him a formal letter of reprimand, but decided not to issue other consequences to Mr. Owen. Dr. Zenga stated that she felt that she had no choice other than to document the issue. The second incident resulted in a long-term suspension for the student. Dr. Zenga showed a great deal of patience in dealing with Mr. Owen, a tenured teacher. Dr. Zenga met with Mr. Owen again and decided to only give him a written reprimand and not pursue further disciplinary action. Mr. Owen violated district policy twice by asking students for a weapon. It was also the second time that students were given consequences based on a request made by Mr. Owen. When the third incident occurred, Dr. Zenga decided to seek advice from Human Resources and the school board attorney. Together they decided to pursue steps toward a Last Chance Agreement for Mr. Owen. Dr. Zenga shared the importance of making difficult decisions along the way to confront a teacher and to document concerns about how a teacher's actions had placed students in compromising positions.

Dr. Zenga further stated,

> What I have noticed about other leaders is that they don't make the small decisions to hold teachers accountable, not in a malicious way, but that makes the decisions harder. In most cases, I am protecting the teacher, because if a parent complains, I can say I took action so the parent doesn't go off and hire a lawyer. It is hard to hold people accountable. Intentions were not bad, but impact was. That is the challenge—to make the small decisions along the way. It would have been easier to say, "Don't do that again," especially when you have a teacher that kids like. I liked him. He was a young personable guy I liked. My major work has been around the achievement gap. He was a voice supporting that work, but at the same time, I have to hold everyone to the standards regardless of whether they are my detractors. By the time I got to the end, it was easy. If there were previous egregious situations, nothing was documented in his file. I knew for his own sake that I had to make those decisions. Those decisions put students in very compromising situations. I made the decision to hold him accountable and to document that. That is a macro decision I have made, when a teacher does something egregious, but in most cases, it will be a letter in their file that won't see the light of day. But in this case once it came out, I had the documentation.

3. Although consequences should be issued for students carrying knives and drugs on campus, this did not prevent parents from raising legitimate questions about the reason students were searched. Given the violation of school committee policy, Dr. Zenga was obliged to assign disciplinary consequences to the students.

4. Dr. Zenga mentioned that although it was difficult, she believed that she was protecting her teacher by documenting her concerns. If she had not taken action, she believed parents would have pursued litigation.

Dr. Zenga reiterated that sometimes painful decisions have to be made that are in the best interest of teachers. If unchecked, Mr. Owen would have been allowed to believe that his behavior was acceptable. Mr. Owen violated district policy on possession of a weapon and subjected students to harsh physical treatment and the display of vulgar sexual content in a classroom without consulting parents or the school principal. Dr. Zenga did not ignore flagrant behavior. She monitored, documented, and when appropriate consulted Human Resources and the school attorney. She also exercised patience. Mr. Owen was a well-liked tenured teacher. Dr. Zenga moved deliberately and chose to avoid rushing to propose termination. She methodically communicated in writing and in person with the teacher, and after several warnings had been issued over a period of 2 years, she moved to offer termination or resignation. Not all the incidents were related, but Mr. Owen's actions showed a pattern of poor judgment with students and a disregard for district policy. Because Dr. Zenga chose to confront the teacher each time, when it became evident that Mr. Owen needed to be terminated or resign, there was sufficient evidence in his file to support her decision. Mr. Owen resigned the spring following the fourth incident.

Chapter 7

Resolution: Case Study #6: Mandatory School Move

1. The first decision Ms. Cantrell made was to make sure that teachers, students, and parents were informed. Ms. Cantrell chose to bring the students in for a full assembly and to tell them that she had not made the decision to move the school to another part of the city. She also told her students that the details of the move were still uncertain, but she wanted to communicate with them about next steps.

2. Ms. Cantrell agreed to send out the letter that stated that the decision to move had been collaborative, but decided not to sign it. Ms. Cantrell made a bold decision to challenge her superintendent given that the statement about collaboration was untrue. Tensions mounted between Ms. Cantrell and her superintendent over Ms. Cantrell's decision to meet with her students before the move was officially announced. Ms. Cantrell decided that she wanted to be the one to tell her students about the move. She wanted them to hear it from her first.

3. Ms. Cantrell contacted her city councilor, and the situation became really complicated. The councilor was willing to defend the elementary school that was being forced out of its building so that Torbay Kent High School could move in. The councilor was not willing, however, to come between Torbay Kent High School and the school department.

4. Ms. Cantrell shared that as she was navigating this situation, she had to determine when to push, how to push, and when to draw

the line in the sand. She also grappled with when to go public and when to be private. If it is clear that political forces that include a powerful, long-standing mayor are supportive of the move, it may not be the political fight to engage in. Principals are often faced with decisions about how to interact with central office supervisors and superintendents especially when inaccurate information is shared publically in an effort to convince the public that a collaborative decision-making process was followed. It is politically risky to disagree publically or privately with a superintendent, particularly about an initiative that the superintendent is promoting, which in this case was the moving of several district schools. Ms. Cantrell chose some politically neutral ground, in that she elected not to fight the move, though she sought out political support from a city councilor before reaching that decision. She also chose not to sign the letter that stated she had collaborated on the decision, but she did not cross a line by refusing to mail the letter. Instead, she complied with the superintendent's request to mail the unrevised letter, but Ms. Cantrell communicated that she would not sign it. In the end, though she faced some tense times with the superintendent, within a couple of years following the move, the superintendent retired and Ms. Cantrell, a long-standing principal in the district, remained in her position as principal of Torbay Kent High School.

List of Tables

List of Case Studies

Glossary

Connect Ed: Electronic mass notification system that can be utilized in K–12 settings to notify families, staff, and others about pertinent school information or to provide updates in an emergency situation. Messages can be sent within a few minutes by phone, text, e-mail, or social media.

Core Values: Fundamental beliefs or guiding principles of an institution or individual that influence behavior.

Culturally Responsive Instruction: Instruction that makes meaningful connections to the diverse backgrounds of classroom students while emphasizing rigorous curricula and high expectations for achievement.

EOCs: The End of Course (EOC) is an exam distributed to students as part of a mandatory state assessment system. In some states, the EOCs are in Math, English, Social Studies, and Science and are taken by students in ninth to twelfth grades.

EVAAS: The Education Value-Added Assessment System allows educators to identify individual student growth and progress over time. In North Carolina, the customized assessment system is used to evaluate student learning and individual educator effectiveness.

Exceptional Education: Exceptional is used synonymously with special education. Exceptional education is instruction that is individually designed to address the specific needs of a child with a disability.

Heuristic Decision Making: Davis (2004) defines heuristic decision making as cutting "problems down to size by chunking patterns of information into easily managed pieces, or rules of thumb. By rules of thumb it is meant that information is organized mentally via predetermined meta-rules that are category based and whole pattern in structure" (p. 631).

Individualized Education Program (IEP): An IEP is a plan that specifies the classification of services that a child is eligible to receive based on his or her disability. The IEP is a legal instrument that includes goals, objectives, and accommodations.

Manifestation Determination: When the disciplinary consequence for a special education student includes the possibility of an alternative placement, suspension, or expulsion, a manifestation determination is conducted to determine the appropriate consequence and to assess whether the student's disability is a mitigating factor. The questions asked consider whether the behaviors are a manifestation of the disability of the student.

METCO: The METCO Program is a voluntary desegregation program that receives funding from the State of Massachusetts. At present, the program serves 3,300 minority students in 33 suburban Boston school districts and 4 districts outside of Springfield. Students are transported on a daily basis from their home in either Boston or Springfield to a neighboring suburban school. METCO Program staff coordinate placement/orientation and implement plans for the recognition and academic achievement of minority students. Additionally METCO staff create projects/systems that help urban students adjust to a suburban community and organize staff development.

NAEP: The National Assessment of Educational Progress, or the Nation's Report card, includes uniform standardized assessments of our nation's children in Reading, Math, Science, Writing, the Arts, Civics, Economics, Geography, U.S. History, and Technology and Engineering Literacy.

School Board: The governing board of a local school district that sets policy for the district. Some states utilize the term School Committee while others use School Board.

School Committee: The governing board of a local school district that sets policy for the district. Some states utilize the term School Committee while others use School Board.

Special Education: In some of the states where principals were interviewed, the term special education was utilized more frequently, in others, exceptional children is the acceptable term. Exceptional education is instruction that is individually designed to address the specific needs of a child with a disability.

Test Item Deconstruction: This approach to curriculum alignment begins with "publically released test items and deconstruct(s) (break(s) them into smaller analytical pieces) to discern the level of cognitive ability, the format and the type of content" (English, 2006, p. 42).

Weingarten Rights: The right to have a union representative attend an investigatory interview.

Index

A SAGE Company

Corwin is committed to improving education for all learners by publishing books and other professional development resources for those serving the field of PreK–12 education. By providing practical, hands-on materials, Corwin continues to carry out the promise of its motto: **"Helping Educators Do Their Work Better."**